# THERE'S A
# CRACK
# IN YOUR
# ARMOR

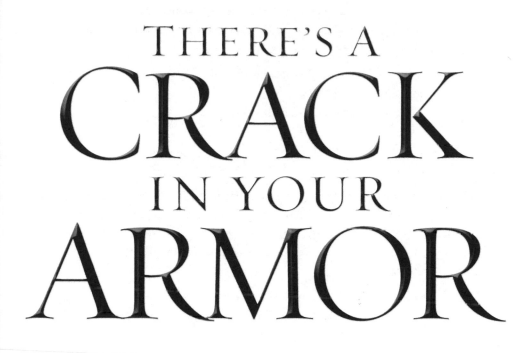

# THERE'S A
# CRACK
# IN YOUR
# ARMOR

## PERRY STONE

CHARISMA
HOUSE

Most CHARISMA HOUSE BOOK GROUP products are available at special quantity discounts for bulk purchase for sales promotions, premiums, fund-raising, and educational needs. For details, write Charisma House Book Group, 600 Rinehart Road, Lake Mary, Florida 32746, or telephone (407) 333-0600.

THERE'S A CRACK IN YOUR ARMOR by Perry Stone
Published by Charisma House
Charisma Media/Charisma House Book Group
600 Rinehart Road
Lake Mary, Florida 32746
www.charismahouse.com

Unless otherwise noted, all Scripture quotations are from the New King James Version of the Bible. Copyright © 1979, 1980, 1982 by Thomas Nelson, Inc., publishers. Used by permission.

Scripture quotations marked AMP are from the Amplified Bible. Old Testament copyright © 1965, 1987 by the Zondervan Corporation. The Amplified New Testament copyright © 1954, 1958, 1987 by the Lockman Foundation. Used by permission.

Scripture quotations marked KJV are from the King James Version of the Bible.

Scripture quotations marked NIV are from the Holy Bible, New International Version. Copyright © 1973, 1978, 1984, International Bible Society. Used by permission.

Cover design by Justin Evans
Design Director: Bill Johnson

Visit the author's website at www.voe.org.

Library of Congress Cataloging-in-Publication Data:
An application to register this book for cataloging has been submitted
to the Library of Congress.
International Standard Book Number: 978-1-62136-248-7
E-book ISBN: 978-1-62136-249-4

First edition

14 15 16 17 18 — 9 8 7 6 5 4 3 2 1
Printed in the United States of America

# Contents

*Introduction*

# The UNEXPECTED CRACK ATTACK

T HAT PARTICULAR DAY INITIATED AN UNPLANNED AND unexpected shocking message no parent ever wants to hear. The family was a strong Christian family and members of a local church where one of my ministry board members, Gary Sears, pastors. The young son of this family was on his way to church, where he worked in the children's ministry, and he was near the time of his high school graduation. While driving, he suddenly hit a wet spot, spinning the car out of control and colliding into a tree. The physical injuries were serious, and the young man was rushed to the hospital with life-threatening injuries. The reports looked bleak and hopeless. The doctor informed the mother that her son would be brain dead. Despite what she saw and heard, this mother of faith began writing healing scriptures, posting them in his room and on the marker board. She prayed, quoted Scripture, and began decreeing that her son would not be brain dead, but he would live and return to a normal life.

---

After some time one of her friends who worked in the medical field came to her and said, "I know you are believing and trusting for him to be healed and normal, but the reality is your son will never be the same, and if he comes through it, he will be probably be a vegetable."

Pastor Gary heard these words, and he observed her countenance and realized her faith level was dropping. That is when Gary said to the mother, "I know that what has been said to you has put a *crack in your armor.*" He then said, "I will stand over you and stand in the gap of that crack in that armor until you have the strength to get your faith back!" The pastor then began to pray the same prayers and confess the same promises from Scripture for which the mother was believing and confessing. Eventually the mother regained her strength to believe and sealed the *crack of doubt* in her shield of faith. Today the same young man has graduated—not just from high school, but also from college with a degree, and is working a job! The only evidence of his previous accident is a slight limp and a few minor things.

Have you experienced an unplanned and unexpected *crack attack* where the trial was so devastating that it weakened your confidence and faith? How many times during your lifetime have you ascended and stood tall on the hill of faith, believing for a good report for a nearly impossible or life-threatening situation, but then you heard a negative report resisting a good outcome or you saw a faith-killing circumstance with your eyes that dashed you from the height of believing to the abyss of despair, like a dreaded avalanche overtaking a skier on a snow-covered mountain? Suddenly you are buried under the burden of doubt and the weight of: "What if it doesn't happen?" "What if it is not God's will?" "What if I believe and get the opposite?" "What if my prayer doesn't get answered?" The what-ifs initiate a slow process of cracking your shield of faith, allowing the small darts of doubt, fear, or unbelief to enter your heart (Eph. 6:16).

The Almighty has provided believers a special *God gear*—a spiritual armor often identified by scholars as the *armor of God* (Eph. 6:13–18). This battle gear equips the believer to enter a full range of combat conditions and engage the adversary, using offensive weapons to attack and numerous defensive weapons to protect oneself from various types of arrows. The success of this gear is dependent upon the believer's *knowledge of the weapons* and insight into the numerous *warfare strategies* of the adversary. You must know how to defend yourself using the gear God has provided. What many believers are not aware of is that despite the strength and durability of God's warfare gear, there are breaks, cracks, and weaknesses that can and do occasionally come, and we must know how to respond and "stand" with battered armor. (See chapter 7, "What to Do With Your Battered Armor.") If you have been engaged in a physical, mental, or spiritual battle, this book will be your resource strategy weapon to bring victory into your situation!

# Chapter 1

# A REVELATION OF
# YOUR GOD GEAR

IN THE NEW TESTAMENT ERA TIME OF CHRIST AND THE APOS-
tles, the spiritual teachers used practical, everyday persons,
places, objects, and real-life examples to help their listeners and
readers understand and visualize spiritual truths and concepts. A
few common examples used through the New Testament are:

- *Farming*—illustrations of farming such as planting,
protecting, and harvesting grains and fruits (Matt.
13:18–32)

- *Fishing*—catching men, mending nets, and dealing
with storms (Matt. 4:18–20; 13:47–50)

- *Running*—a foot race, winning the prize, not giving
up, and laying aside weights and sins (Heb. 12:1–2)

- *Warring*—a soldier who is equipped with armor to fight and defeat enemies (Eph. 6:10–20)

Perhaps you enjoy those promises of reaping and sowing and prefer to remain in the farming scriptures. For those who like athletic activities, you can relate to the run-the-race admonition in Hebrews 12:1–2, because you desire to win the prize. However, if you are an active Christian, you are to be continually prepared for a surprise spiritual conflict that attacks your health, wealth, or family—similar to the assault leveled against Job. (See Job 1–2.) We must all understand that this conflict is the battle of the ages, and each soul that falls in battle, wounded and unable to stand, is a victory in the kingdom of darkness.

*Anyone who is a Christian is also a soldier.* After ministering to hundreds of thousands of believers, I have observed four basic types of soldiers in the body of Christ:

1. First are those who know *nothing* about the armor of God. They live from one battle to the next, survive from one beating to the next, and anticipate one defeat to the next. They are the ones who have a desire to serve God but their conflicts bring a defeatist mentality as they are uncertain *how* to win in a conflict.

2. The second category is those who know something *about* the armor of God but *refuse to wear it*. To them Ephesians 6:13–18 is a beautiful poetic passage penned by an apostle in prison. However, their belief is that we must all learn how to deal with our own problems in our own wisdom and strength and not over concern ourselves with some form of *invisible spiritual warfare*.

3. The third category is the soldiers who *pick and choose* their protection, wearing some but not all of the armor. They enjoy a spiritual victory occasionally, answered prayer from time to time, a healing during certain seasons, but they often leave areas of their lives exposed to the darts of the enemy. They may attend church for many years, but suddenly they drop off the radar and no one sees them in the Sunday services because they were hit by the enemy in an unprotected moment.

4. The fourth category of Christian warrior is those Christians who *wear the entire armor* of God and actually know what it represents and how to use it. These Christians have battles just like everyone else, but despite battles and wars, they continue to survive and thrive even during raging conflicts.

The Book of Ephesians was the first major letter that Paul wrote from prison. The Roman prisons were often a dungeon in a building of stone, with the worst living conditions imaginable. The most politically dangerous men were often chained between two guards, as indicated in the case with Peter:

> And when Herod was about to bring him out, that night Peter was sleeping, bound with two chains between two soldiers; and the guards before *the door were keeping the prison.*
> —ACTS 12:6, EMPHASIS ADDED

In Paul's letter to Timothy he mentioned his "chain" (2 Tim. 1:16), a reference to Paul's imprisonment in Rome. Throughout his arrests, as recorded in Acts, Paul was often placed in chains (Acts 21:33; 26:29). Paul did not spend time sulking and questioning why God allowed him to be arrested. Instead he wrote several letters from prison, including the epistle to the church at Ephesus, called the Book of Ephesians in the New Testament.

It is interesting that Paul would write a detailed discourse on the spiritual battle of a believer against demonic rebels to the Ephesian believers. Ephesus was the fourth greatest city in the world, following Rome, Alexandria, and Antioch. It was the largest city in Asia Minor, with stadiums, schools of philosophy, massive temples to idols, and gyms. Built with a major seaport, the city attracted many visitors and tourists. Among the common destinations in Ephesus was the temple of the Greek goddess Artemis, which the Romans called *Diana*. The city was also known for its prostitutions (including temple prostitutes), public bathhouses, and idol worship, which dominated the city. Crowds of more than ten thousand people often filled the stadiums for the gladiator fights.[1]

This was the setting Paul had observed when reminding the saints that their battle was not against flesh and blood but against satanic spirits ruling in high places (Eph. 6:12).

Paul was very familiar with Roman soldiers, Roman guards, and their military training, equipment, and methods of battle. In this prison setting he penned the famous discourse on the armor of God. The Book of Ephesians can be divided into three distinct sections: the *work* of God in the life of a Christian (chapters 1–3), the *walk* of the Christian (chapters 4–5), and the *warfare* of the Christian (chapter 6).

> Finally, my brethren, be strong in the Lord and in the power of His might. Put on the whole armor of God, that you may be able to stand against the wiles of the devil. For we do not wrestle against flesh and blood, but against principalities, against powers, against the rulers of the darkness of this age, against spiritual hosts of wickedness in the heavenly places. Therefore take up the whole armor of God, that you may be able to withstand in the evil day, and having done all, to stand.
>
> Stand therefore, having girded your waist with truth,

having put on the breastplate of righteousness, and having shod your feet with the preparation of the gospel of peace; above all, taking the shield of faith with which you will be able to quench all the fiery darts of the wicked one. And take the helmet of salvation, and the sword of the Spirit, which is the word of God; praying always with all prayer and supplication in the Spirit, being watchful to this end with all perseverance and supplication for all the saints.

—EPHESIANS 6:10–18

Being a Roman citizen and seeing Roman soldiers daily who occupied Israel and observing them closely while being imprisoned, Paul chose the military metaphor of the Roman soldier's armor as the war dress for the believer.

## THE LOIN BELT

His first selection was the *loin belt* (Eph. 6:14, KJV), which was called *balteus* in the early Roman Empire and *cingulum militare* in latter times.[2] These belts were narrow and decorated with bronze plates all the way around. They included five leather straps hanging over the lower half of the front of the body. With it being a belt of truth, I am reminded of the fivefold ministry gifts—pastor, evangelist, prophet, apostle, and teacher—that present God's truth to the church. The soldier's belt was later used for the soldier to attach his sword and a small shield. The belt also held other parts of the armor in place and was used to tie or bind up the garments (called girding up the loins in 2 Kings 4:29, KJV) so a soldier would not trip when going to battle. It was also used to display awards and metals for heroism in battle. This first piece of equipment, "truth," holds all things together! If your faith and hope are not grounded in biblical truth, then what you believe will eventually fall apart during a spiritual battle.

## THE BREASTPLATE

The soldier's *breastplate* (Eph. 6:14) is called in Greek the *thorax*, which can literally mean, a "heart protector." The Roman soldier's breastplate was made up of small metal plates tied together in a fashion similar to how roof tiles are placed on a roof. These individual strips helped create flexibility and allowed the soldier to have mobility in battle. The breastplate was designed to protect the vital organs of the soldier's body. The purpose of the metal was to deflect the blows from the enemy's swords and other weapons, protecting especially the chest and heart region. Paul called this "the breastplate of righteousness." Righteousness is the quality of being *right or just* in God's eyes and doing things God's way. Righteousness is imparted in the heart and spirit, and it must be protected from the lies and deception of the enemy.

This breastplate was placed over the shoulders to protect both the front and back of the soldier. The bottom of the breastplate was tied to the belt. Notice that *righteousness* must be tied to the belt of *truth*, as there is no righteousness unless we receive the Word of God, which is the word of truth (John 17:17). I have often heard that the soldier's back was the only area that had no protection on the Roman breastplate. After research, and after purchasing an entire replica of the Roman armor for a sermon illustration, I discovered this was incorrect. Thin metal sheets also formed a protective covering around the back rib cage, and the entire breastplate was tied together by leather straps in the back. These individual and layered metal strips gave freedom of movement to the soldier in times of battle. The spiritual application is that righteousness does not mean to be rigid or self-righteous or legalistic, but righteousness is a joyful, heart-filled expression of a life redeemed by God. His righteousness covering your heart brings freedom of moment to enjoy God's blessings and freedom of movement to wage a good warfare.

## THE SOLDIER'S SHOES

The solder's shoes were important. The shoes were actually *sandals* made of leather with straps that wrapped around the calves up to the knees. Due to the open-air design and the soft leather, it enabled the soldiers to walk up to twenty-five miles a day without blisters or developing fungi. A strip of metal was built in each shoe to provide stability. Under both shoes were metal studs of two sizes, some were small and others longer on the shoes, depending upon the terrain where the battle was being waged. These provided traction for walking, running, and standing for long hours when fighting. These spikes were excellent when standing on a hill or if the ground was slippery, as the spikes dug into the ground, assisting the solder in his ability to stand without slipping and falling. Part of the armor also included metal greaves that attached to the front of the ankles and the knees, providing protection to the shins and knees. Believers are to be prepared to take "the gospel of peace" (Eph. 6:15) to all people under all circumstances and not be knocked off our feet by the opposition we may encounter.

## THE SHIELD OF FAITH

Paul admonished, "Above all, taking the shield of faith" (v. 16). *Above all* means "over and above all, take the shield of faith." There were two types of Roman shields. One smaller round shield, called the *aspis,* was used mostly for display and was about the size of a large pizza; it was hooked to the loin belt and was used in parades held after a war victory. The larger shield was used for one-on-one conflict and battles. The word *shield* here is *thureon* and refers to a large shield with the oblong shape of a door, about four and one-half feet high, with a curved shape.

These large shields are the ones we see in the movies of the Roman times. In a battle five hundred soldiers were deployed in a line—shoulder to shoulder—facing the enemy. The shields could be thrust against the body of the enemy to throw them off balance, as the front of the battle shield had a sharp metal point called the *umbo* constructed in the center. After the shield was withdrawn, the sword of the soldier was used to thrust through the body of the enemy. The constant thrust of the shield and the sword could eventually disorient the enemy. When Christ was tempted for forty days by Satan in the Judean wilderness, He quoted three scriptures from the Book of Deuteronomy to counter the three sharp arrows of Satan (Matt. 4:1–10).

The large individual shields of these soldiers could be joined side by side as soldiers stood shoulder to shoulder, forming a protective wall in battle. They were also used to *cover the heads* of the soldiers, forming a covering like a tortoise shell. This position was called the *testudo* and was used when the enemy soldiers dropped large rocks from the walls of a city being invaded. Just as soldiers joined together in battle, believers must not fight alone, but join our faith with others, as the more shields in battle, the more faith is released to bring victory!

Likewise, Christians can link their shields of faith together when confronting social issues that are contrary to the Bible. One lone Christian with his one shield has less protection from an onslaught of arrows than if he or she were to join with other Christians and link their shield to the faith shields of others. The enemy can throw all the arrows, spears, and fiery darts he wants, causing us to feel the hit but not the pain or the injury, as we are protected behind a wall of shields and undergirded by the faith of God's army. In Roman times, if a person attempted to jump over the soldiers' shields, that person would feel the cut from a double-edged sword in the hand of the one bearing the shield.

## ONE BODY

I believe the body of Christ is lacking in the area of uniting their faith as one. Paul said we are to work "together" (Eph. 1:10;

2:5–6, 22). Paul uses the word *one* when speaking of Christ's body, the church (Eph. 2:15–16, 18; 4:4–6). We are instructed to be united in our faith. The Bible says that there is "one Lord, one faith, one baptism" (Eph. 4:5). But there have been men who have taught or emphasized one truth and made it *the sole truth*, splitting away from other Christian groups to surround themselves with a following who accept their single doctrine as solo truth. So, everyone has their own denominational or biblical interpretative shield. One person is standing behind their *Pentecostal* shield. Another may be stooped behind his *Catholic* shield, and yet another may boast, "Here is my *Baptist* shield." *The problem is that we end up fighting each other over doctrine, instead of fighting the real enemy of us all—Satan and his demonic rebels!*

While the adversary is leading people into bondages like alcoholism, pornography, drugs, child abuse, and fornication, Christians are linking our shields around doctrinal issues such as what is the true baptismal formula, or whether certain gifts have ceased and others are still operational, or whether miracles can occur today or were strictly for the first century. Some even make a major doctrine on not permitting musical instruments in a church worship setting. It is frustrating to see so many people focusing on personal interpretations and not on helping others overcoming evil inclinations. There is friction over the style of music and types of songs being sung on Sunday morning. Sunday morning is still the most segregated day of the week in America.

If a doctrinal issue or interpretation has no bearing upon our salvation or eternal destination, then the body of Christ needs to grow up and quit beating a horse that has no legs, meaning stop dividing the church over issues that will carry us nowhere but into a field of division where we are all hiding under our little lights under our man-made denominational bushels. Instead of spreading out over the city trying to hold down the fort in our local churches, keeping the saints in and the devil out, we should start linking our shields to have a greater impact in the community and the city. God does not want us to be independent (standing alone) or codependent (unable to stand without someone's help); He wants us to be *interdependent*, meaning we need one another standing shoulder to shoulder to engage the adversary.

The church by and large is sitting back while we allow 15 percent of the population—the liberal media, college professors, and press—to undermine our faith and brainwash the next generation with their ungodly propaganda. Evolution, abortion, and the destruction of traditional marriage are deadly tares in the wheat field and poison in the drinking water. Yet the saints battle over the style of music on Sunday while their children and grandchildren sleep in at home with a hangover from Saturday night's party.

It seems like the only prayer Jesus prayed that has not yet been answered is recorded in John chapter 17. Twice He prayed that we would be one just as He and the Father are one (vv. 11, 21). Jesus is coming back for a bride who is without spot or wrinkle, and we must be one to be that bride. We must learn to link our shields of faith together and become one for the end-time battle.

In addition to linking our shields of faith together, we all need to have the full-size shield of faith. The Bible says that there are five different levels of faith, or different sizes of shields.

------------------------------------------------------

## Five Levels of Faith

1. No faith (Mark 4:40)

2. Little faith (Matt. 8:26)

3. Weak faith (Rom. 4:19)

4. Strong faith (Rom. 4:20)

5. Great faith (Matt. 8:10)

------------------------------------------------------

Strong faith and great faith are strong and great shields!

Often believers will confuse faith with a certain emotional feeling they receive in God's presence. It is important to point out that faith and emotions are two different things. Some people confuse excited emotions for faith. For example, they go to a meeting and the place is packed out. Everyone is really excited, so they think, "Yeah! God is going to do something here tonight! Just look at all those excited people!" Then that same person will go to a meeting where there are only fifty people and think, "Doesn't look like much is going to happen here tonight." We must remember Christ's words: "For where two or three are gathered together in My name, I am there in the midst of them" (Matt. 18:20).

Someone once asked me if I thought people are actually being healed in a particular television minister's meetings. They asked because they see some people who do not seem to be all that excited after they say God healed them. I said, "There are two groups. One group is healed and totally shocked, are often jumping and crying. The other group is from mainline denominations and actually expected the healing to occur; they are not as surprised and simply are grateful from their heart."

For example, when I was eighteen years old, I was preaching a revival in Carmi, Illinois. One night I called for a prayer line to minister to the needs of people. I recall a distinguished Baptist woman who came for prayer. She was deaf in one ear and partially deaf in the other ear. I prayed for her and commanded the "deaf spirit" to come out (Mark 9:25). Suddenly her deaf ear popped open! She could suddenly hear completely in both ears, and she said, "Wow, my ears just popped open and I can hear again. Praise the Lord! Thank you." And then she quietly walked away. I was anticipating that at any moment she would either break out into a Baptist breakdance or run down the aisle! I asked the Lord why she didn't get all that excited. I sensed the Holy Spirit saying, "Because she knew that when you prayed, she would be healed, thus she was not surprised." She had a word (*rhema*) from the Word (*logos*) of God, and faith comes when you hear the *rhema* (Word) of God!

## ANOINTING YOUR SHIELDS

The Romans called the large shields the *scutum*. Each was built with two layers of wooden strips (similar to plywood) laid at right angles to each other and heated so that they could be pressed into a curved shape. After being formed, it was covered with six layers of animal hide. A soldier had to maintain his shield by caring for the leather animal skin covering, which could become dry. The danger of a dry shield was that the covering would become brittle and vulnerable to fire. To prevent a dry shield, the soldier carried olive oil and would rub the surface of the shield with oil. The prophet Isaiah instructed men to, "Anoint the shield" (Isa. 21:5), or to prepare them for battle. The oil represents the Holy Spirit, as oil was used to anoint spiritual leaders in the Bible, and afterward the Holy Spirit would come upon them (1 Sam. 16:13). Our faith must be anointed, or energized by the fresh oil of the Holy Spirit, to effectively quench or put out the fiery arrows of the devil!

Each Christian must keep his or her shield anointed. As I stated above, a Roman soldier would rub olive oil into his shield to keep the leather from drying out. Just as drying out caused the shield to be more vulnerable to a fiery dart, dry churches produce dry shields and leave the Christians more vulnerable to a hot attack from the adversary. If no practical applications of the Word are taught, and the atmosphere is dead and boring, it is a *dry* church. Our shields must be regularly anointed by solid and practical teaching. I have discovered that if I exercise faith without an anointing, then more mental toil is required, and the human mind will wage war against the spirit man.

Since oil represents the anointing of the Holy Spirit, how do we anoint our shields? Jude verse 20 says, "But you, beloved, building yourselves up on your most holy faith, praying in the Holy Spirit." The apostle Paul also knew this truth and regularly prayed in the Spirit (1 Cor. 14:15, 18); that is, he prayed in the supernatural prayer language the Holy Spirit had imparted to him. This is called "praying with the Spirit." Notice that you must *build up yourself in the faith by praying in the prayer language of the Spirit.* Since your faith is your shield, you build up the strength of your shield by the prayer language of the Spirit; then you anoint your shield through the anointing of the Spirit.

This generation seems to have difficulty resisting sin. When observing our spiritual fathers, we know they too experienced temptation in the time of their generation. However, they seemed to have a greater resistance to evil and walked disciplined as they desired to walk pure and not trip up spiritually. As we glean from their stories, their ability to face temptation and overcome was based in the fact that they despised sin. To them, sin was like a cancer, and once one cell was in the body, it could bring death. Therefore they didn't think twice about it, didn't reason with it, and didn't put their toe in the water of temptation to see if they would like to take a dip.

The second key to overcoming was their prayer life. The fathers of the faith didn't wait until Sunday morning arrived to communicate with God. They prayed daily, they prayed often, and at times they prayed long! When faith was lacking, they prayed in the Spirit to strengthen their faith shield.

My father told a story of when he was a young unmarried minister, and he traveled with his uncle, Rufus Dunford, who had a spiritual gift of faith and working of miracles in his ministry. (See 1 Corinthians 12:7–10.) One night in Beef Hide, Kentucky, Dad saw Rufus pray for a young boy born with a club foot. The lad literally walked on the outer ball of his foot and had never run or played with other children. That night Rufus prayed, and nothing happened. He told the church to fast and pray, and he told the fellow to come back the next night. Dad said he and Rufus fasted and spent the entire day on a high mountain praying for several hours. That night, when prayer was offered, the Lord wrought a miracle, and the foot went straight as all people in the church saw the miracle. For the first time in his life the boy ran around the church, crying and laughing. I regret to confess it, but our generation, after the first prayer, would have patted the fellow on the head and said, "Keep praying, because you never know what God will do!" When the shields become dry, the oil of the Spirit is necessary to inspire our faith.

A strong shield of faith requires a prayer covering. One of the biblical types of prayer is to pray "in the Spirit," or as we say today, "Pray in the prayer language of the Holy Spirit," which is the language a believer received upon being baptized in the Holy Spirit (Acts 2:1–4; 10:44–46; 19:1–7). When praying in the Holy Spirit, our spirit is praying (1 Cor. 14:14), and our spirit is speaking to God (v. 2). Romans 8:26–28 reveals that the Holy Spirit makes intercession for us, and in Jude 20 we build ourselves up in the faith! The strength of your shield and its ability to stop the flying arrows of the adversary are based upon the amount of biblical teaching and knowledge you have received and the level of a prayer life in which you are walking. A new convert is like a soldier going through boot camp. Often young, future soldiers will think, "What have I gotten myself into?" They miss home, they miss their old friends, and at times wish they could quit and go back to their old way of life. However, after forging relationships and team building with other future soldiers, and catching the vision of their role as a defender of freedom, they survive boot camp and learn how to dress for the battle and use their weapons to defend themselves and their fellow soldiers in a real conflict.

THE TYPES OF DARTS OF THE ENEMY

The shield of faith is used to "quench all the fiery darts of the wicked one" (Eph. 6:16). In the Roman period there were three types of arrows that could be chosen in a battle. The first was the normal arrow tipped with a sharp, pointed metal arrowhead, the most common in war. The second was a normal-looking arrow with the metal tip dipped in a pitch, tar-like substance, lit aflame, then shot from the bow against wooden frames or wooden structures. When hitting its target, this arrow caused a small fire (a *burning*) that damaged what it struck and distracted the opponent. The third type of arrow was formed by filling the stem of the arrow with a combustible substance, lighting the arrowhead, and sending the arrow in the direction of the enemy. Once the arrow struck the target, the impact split the stem of the arrow, scattering the combustible liquid and causing the fire on the tip to spread onto the object the arrow had struck. This was a "fiery arrow." Also, there were "fire darts," which were long spear shafts with three-foot iron heads that were set on fire; these darts were so powerful they could thrust through armor.[3] The "fiery darts" (or arrows) of Satan are the sudden thoughts the adversary shoots into your mind, setting the imagination on fire as the mental images, thoughts, or whispering words burn into your conscience, and you are overwhelmed by the burning sensation or, at times, images or thoughts pouring into your mind. It is the Word of God and confidence in Christ that strengthen your shield, preventing the sudden *fire* from moving out of your thoughts into actions. All forms of temptation must be resisted, or the thoughts become deeds, the deeds sin, and the sin, bondage. Paul instructed believers to "[cast] down imaginations" (2 Cor. 10:5, KJV) and every wrong thought that attempts to become superior to God's knowledge. When you cast images down and out, then you have successfully *deflected* a dart with your shield of faith.

Some mental thoughts can be like wood thrown on a burning fire—they keep the mind distracted with *stuff* that oppresses and wears a person down. The following sidebar lists some of these mental attacks.

------------------------------------------------

## Mental Attacks From Satan

1. Mental attack of fear (2 Tim. 1:7)

2. The mental attack of lust of the flesh (1 John 2:16)

3. The mental dart of sudden anger (Matt. 5:22)

4. The mental pressure of oppression (Acts 10:38)

5. The mental feeling of condemnation from sin (1 John 3:20–22)

------------------------------------------------

Living in a human body is a guarantee that sooner or later these darts, like a falling asteroid, will head in your direction. These darts must never stick in the mind, but they must be stopped the moment they begin flying and circling your head. I have often said, "You can't keep the birds from flying, but you can keep them from building a nest on your head." *You can't prevent satanic arrows from coming in your direction, but you can deflect them when they arrive.*

## THE SOLDIER'S HELMET

In Ephesians 6:17 Paul mentions the necessity of a helmet of salvation. The Roman soldier's helmet was made from a copper-iron alloy. These helmets were used to protect the head; they also bore on them the army's insignia or symbol. The top was bowl shaped and protected the top of the head from blows. There was a neck guard connected to the back of the helmet to protect the back of the neck, and a brow guard that protruded out of the top near the forehead guarded from frontal downward blows. Two metal pieces that were like movable flaps were attached to the left and right side of the helmet, designed to protect the cheekbones and the jaws from any impacts to the face. Thus, the helmet protected the head and front of the face from all directions—the side, front, and back!

When we speak of salvation or being saved, salvation begins with a person's *repentance,* which means to turn or to change your thinking. Once we *repent,* our minds must be guarded from the mental blows and darts of the enemy. When a negative or sinful thought reaches our mind, it can be pulled down and removed by disciplining our minds and thoughts, training our minds to react to God's Word. We require movement with our jaws to produce words. The cheek guards on the helmet, to me, are a part of guarding the words that proceed out of our mouths, for thoughts are transferred to words, and words can produce either life or death (Prov. 18:21).

## THE SWORD OF THE SPIRIT

Paul called the Word of God the "sword of the Spirit" (Eph. 6:17). The sword of the Spirit is the only *offensive* weapon listed in the armor of God, as all of the other pieces either provide protection from the enemy or are intended for use in the rough battle terrain. At the time of Paul's writing, there were four different swords used in the Roman period.

---

### Four Types of Battle Swords

1. The *gladius hispaniensis* ("Spanish sword") was adopted by the Romans after they engaged in a battle in Spain. This sword was designed for use in close combat and for stabbing rather than slashing.[4]

2. The *Pompeii sword* was shorter than the *gladius hispaniensis,* having a double-edged blade with a length

of approximately sixteen inches and a width of two and one-half inches. Four of the Pompeii swords were found during excavations of the ruins of Pompeii, the famous city in Italy destroyed by a volcanic eruption centuries ago.[5]

3. The *cavalry sword* was a long, single-edged sword of iron or steel. The blade was called the *spatha* and averaged twenty-seven inches in length. As the name indicates, this sword was well suited for use by the soldiers that fought while riding on horses (the cavalry).[6]

4. The *machaira sword* was an offensive sword, made of iron. It was two feet long, two-edged, with a sharp tip for stabbing the enemy. The sword could attack an opponent or defend from the enemy's blows. When not in use, the machaira sword was stored in a scabbard that was attached to the loin belt.[7]

-------------------------------------------------

In Ephesians 6:17 the Greek word used is *macharia*. Notice that this offensive weapon was attached to the loin belt. This is significant because we must have our offensive and defensive components of the armor attached to the truth (the loin belt of truth). The truth of God's Word is the support that lifts our sword when in battle and brings rest in times of peace. Scripture declares that the Word of God is "living and powerful, and sharper than any two-edged sword" (Heb. 4:12). Some knives and swords had only one sharp side; however, this sword had two extremely sharp sides; thus it is a "two-edged" sword. In Hebrews 4:12 the word "two-edged" in Greek is *distomos* and is literally, "two mouthed"; *distomos* was used to describe a road or a river that branched out into two directions.[8] On the believer's sword, I suggest that one blade was sharpened when *God spoke* His Word to the prophets, and the second blade is the power released from the written Word of God when *you speak it*...thus two mouths: God's and yours.

In Revelation the words from Christ's mouth are described as a "two-edged sword" (Rev. 1:16; 2:12). When Christ returns to earth to defeat the armies of the Antichrist, He exercises the authority of His words, which release such light and power that the words from His mouth consume the enemies of Israel while they are standing on their feet (Rev. 19:15; 2 Thess. 2:8).

There are also two main Greek words used for "word" in the phrase "word of God," which is found forty-five times in forty-four verses in the New Testament. One Greek word is *logos*, and the other is *rhema*. The word *logos* means, "a saying, a topic, or divine expression; the expression of a thought." The word *rhema* generally means, "an individual, collective and specific utterance," or "that which is spoken, what is uttered in speech and writing."[9] The main difference between the two is that a *rhema* is a word or scripture that the Holy Spirit quickens to your spirit, bringing with it a strong faith to believe and act thereon. According to Paul, "the sword of the Spirit...is the word of God" (Eph. 6:17), and the Greek for "word" here is *rhema*, meaning the words that God quickens to our spirit through the Bible or in your heart. When the Holy Spirit takes a scripture from the printed page into your spirit, suddenly you feel literal faith come alive, and then you have in your possession the sword of the Spirit! The *rhema* word is both an offensive and defensive weapon we can use in battle against the words, devices, and plans of the enemy. W. E. Vine gives one of the best descriptions of a *rhema*:

> The significance of rhema (as distinct from logos) is exemplified in the injunction to take the sword of the Spirit, which is the word of God (Eph. 6:17); here the reference is not to the whole Bible as such, but to the individual scripture which the Spirit brings to our remembrance for use in time of need,

a prerequisite being the regular storing in the mind of the Scripture.[10]

Paul wrote, "So then faith comes by hearing, and hearing by the word of God" (Rom. 10:17). The Greek for "word" in this passage is *rhema*. The in-depth interpretation of this verse can be that faith comes when hearing a *rhema* word that God energizes or quickens to your spirit. *Rhema* is the Greek word used in the following passages for "word":

> But He answered and said, "It is written, 'Man shall not live by bread alone, but by every word that proceeds from the mouth of God.'"
> —MATTHEW 4:4

> But if he will not hear, take with you one or two more, that "by the mouth of two or three witnesses every word may be established."
> —MATTHEW 18:16

> But Simon answered and said to Him, "Master, we have toiled all night and caught nothing; nevertheless at Your word I will let down the net."
> —LUKE 5:5

> But what does it say? "The word is near you, in your mouth and in your heart" (that is, the word of faith which we preach).
> —ROMANS 10:8

I describe a *rhema* moment as the moment when the Word being read or preached is made alive in your own spirit. Let's picture together ten people sitting on the front row of a church, listening to a message on the subject of deliverance from fear. All are struggling with fear and anxiety. As the minister expounds from Scripture, quoting select verses and breaking down word studies for a practical application, suddenly six of the ten begin to weep, worship, and find their way to the altar for prayer. It is not that they were "emotionally moved" to tears or that they are sad, but faith has risen and their inner spirit is now opened to release the "stuff" that had bound them in fear. The tears are an indication of relief and joy, as they can feel in their spirit a level of faith and confidence that had been missing.

## PETER HAD A *RHEMA* MOMENT

Peter was a professional fisherman and knew the ins and outs of the fishing industry. He knew that at the Sea of Galilee, fisherman fished at night when the cooler weather settled in because the fish moved closer to the surface and could be caught in the nets. When the sun comes up, the fishermen bring in their boats and put up their nets. (The same is true today.) Peter fished "all night" and caught nothing. Jesus had borrowed Peter's boat to stand in and preach to the multitude. (Water effectively carries sound, and the people could actually hear better from Christ in a boat a short distance from shore, as the water carried His voice back to the land.) After the sermon Christ gave Peter a specific word for a specific moment. He said:

> When he stopped speaking, He said to Simon, "Launch out into the deep and let down your nets for a catch."
> —LUKE 5:4

Peter reasoned that despite the fact he was worn out from an all-night fishing trip, at Christ's *word* (the Greek here for "word" being *rhema*), he would take his boat and net back into the water. Christ said to take "nets," and Peter took a single net. Peter soon discovered he needed "nets" and more boats, as the catch was a record breaker! The miracle of fish in the net put Peter under conviction, and he left boats, nets, and his fishing business to become a fisher of men (vv. 8–10). Your *rhema* moment is when you receive a direct word from Scripture or a personal instruction from the Holy Spirit, and what you have read or heard burns into your heart, and your faith becomes energized.

The Scriptures are the sword of the "Spirit," or the weapon of the *Holy* Spirit, as He is the agent who inspired the prophets to pen the Word of God (2 Tim. 3:16; 2 Pet. 1:21). If the Bible is His personal sword, which severs the lies of the enemy, cuts the hardened layers off your heart, and defends you from outward demonic assaults, then it requires the Holy Spirit to be present, as He is the agent of faith. If a minister or his members fight against the operation and manifestation of the Holy Spirit in their local church, then the people will develop a form of Christianity without the dynamic power (2 Tim. 3:5). They will have a *confession* of faith but often lack a *growing* faith, which should accompany spiritual maturity.

As stated, the Word of God is a two-edged sword and operates on two levels: one is defensive and one is offensive. As a defensive weapon, the Word of God defends your heart against lies and deception. It also defends the mind against mental attacks and is a weapon to defend against the power of temptation. It has within its "spiritual DNA" the inherent power to resist, restrain, and rebuke. As an offensive weapon, the Word of God attacks the power and presence of sin as it cuts into the human spirit and begins to extract the sin influence out of your inner man. The Word of God is an offensive weapon to attack sickness, and it becomes the scalpel of the Great Physician to eradicate sickness and disease out of the human body. The Word is also an offensive, protective weapon to guard against thoughts of seduction as it cuts into channels of the mind. The Word of God divides the soul from the spirit (Heb. 4:12), or the carnal mind (the soulish realm) from the spirit man (the spiritual realm). The Word redeems, reconciles, renews, and repairs.

## WHICH LEVEL ARE YOU ON?

Many years ago during a Main Event Camp meeting, I preached my first illustrated sermon, illustrating one of four levels of the Word of God in which the average believer is walking. I illustrated the message using four types of cutting instruments.

### THE POCKETKNIFE LEVEL

There is the pocketknife level of knowing God's Word. Being from the mountains of West Virginia, every young boy in my day was given a pocketknife at an early age. It's something you just carry around in the front pocket of your jeans. In reality, it was seldom used unless we became bored—it was something we pulled out in our spare time. So many believers have Bibles scattered in every room of their home, reminding them they are believers and to *think about God*, but too many only open up the Bible when they are bored with nothing else to do or occasionally in their spare time. When I was a kid, my pocketknife was used when I wanted to take a small tree branch and whittle away. These pocketknife believers will whittle you down to size if you teach something they disagree with, or they will spend time "whittling away" at things that are insignificant with little spiritual benefit. They view the Bible as a simple story book to help put the kids to sleep at night. Some "casual" Christians have a pocketknife mentality as it relates to the Bible. They seldom attend church, unless they are bored on Sunday and decide to drop in and warm a pew.

### BUTTER-KNIFE BELIEVERS

I compare the second level of Christians and their biblical knowledge to a *butter knife*. My wife has two sets of dishes—the everyday dishes used for lunch or dinner with the family, and the special china that is pulled out when company arrives during the holidays. On those special occasions genuine silverware is placed on the main table. I must confess that I love butter. In fact, I like it so much that I could eat it all by itself (but I won't and don't). On special occasions she lays the silver butter knife on the glass dish for the butter lovers.

To me, this level of the Word of God represents those who want a shiny, polished, and politically correct Word that will inspire, bless, and never offend. There are some Christians who would *never* attend a worship service in a church where the worship was verbal, the praise was loud, or the music was being played by a band and not just some pipe organ. There are certainly times to worship with exuberance and times to be still, times to rejoice and times of reverence. However, *reverence is not deadness!* Some congregations declare themselves "reverent Christians," when in reality they are repeating the patterns of the church of Sardis—they "have a name...but you are dead" (Rev. 3:1).

If your level of knowing and using the Word of God is the butter-knife level, then know that a butter knife is only effective on soft butter. Butter-knife Christianity is far too dull to have any impact in cutting away the works of the flesh, the power of temptation, or to defeat your inner enemies. My wife brings out the butter knife only during special occasions, reminding me that some believers are *seasonal Christians*, meaning they show up and show out during special *holiday holy days*, such as traditional celebrations of Easter and Christmas, expressing their "faith" two days out of three hundred sixty-five a year. To these people, church should be polished and short, without any emotional display, and occasional, not weekly.

## MEAT-CLEAVER LEVEL

The third group of believers is the *meat-cleaver* level of Christians. My wife, being a wonderful cook, has numerous types of knives in her kitchen at home and on the youth ranch. This large butcher knife, as some call it, is used to cut the meat from the bone or to cut the bone in half on a large piece of beef. In the Bible the "milk" of the Word is the simplicity of understanding the Bible, which is the level of a babe in Christ or an immature Christian. However, the "meat" of the Word is the strong doctrinal and practical teaching, or what we would say are the *deeper parts* of the Bible (Heb. 5:12–13). The *meat eaters* are those mature believers who have passed beyond the milk and no longer desire the simple basic teaching; they must have deep teaching—something to feed off of and make them think. They must leave the service in awe saying, "Wow," as the message must have mesmerized them, or they feel slighted and half fed. These individuals grow rabbit legs and hop from church to church looking for a *chef* instead of a *pastor,* someone who can cut up the beef, throwing well-done steak on the church grill each Sunday. Their common statement to simple preaching is, "I didn't get fed today."

Since I was age eighteen, my life has been spent studying and researching biblical truths. I have more than seventy-five thousand hours of biblical research, and I enjoy digging out Hebraic prophetic truths related to the Scripture that I was previously unaware of. However, I enjoy all forms of teaching and preaching, and I have never removed myself from the preaching of the simplicity of the Word. For me, no message from God's Word is boring, and foundational truth must be consistently presented. There is a danger in becoming an overly perfected *meat eater only*—a person who becomes spiritually fat on the meat and can become critical of a church or believer who is not on the *same level* of the *deeper knowledge* he or she is experiencing. This becomes pride.

Paul warned the church at Corinth not to allow knowledge and pride to "puff them up." The phrase "puffed up" is the Greek word *phusioo,* which means to inflate or to blow something up. He warned the Corinthian believers of being puffed up five times (1 Cor. 4:6, 18, 19; 5:2; 13:4). The idea is that believers with great understanding and knowledge may tend to allow themselves to have an inflated ego and act superior to those of less understanding. If you enjoy the meat of the Word, never become arrogant in your knowledge and treat others of less understanding as someone feeding on bologna while you chew on fillet.

As a humorous note, years ago I was driving a ministry friend to the airport. This person was seeing up to ten thousand people attend his conferences, whereas we were having about twenty-five hundred in our largest meetings. I jokingly asked, "Why can you get ten thousand at a meeting, and I can't get more than twenty-five hundred?"

Without blinking, he replied, "You are too deep! I am a simple minister using illustrations of life, but you are the Hebrew-prophetic guy, and only a small percent understand the deeper well of knowledge you draw from."

For some time I thought, "I need to preach more simply where everyone understands," yet I knew that my calling was to feed people the in-depth, deeper knowledge of the Word and help them mature and become hungry to learn more from God's inspired Book. Meat is good, but babes will choke to death on strong meat. There is nothing wrong with desiring meat, but there is something wrong when you refuse to listen to someone minister a simple, basic word from God. All of God's Word—the milk and the meat—will help you grow.

## THE TWO-EDGED SWORD LEVEL

The fourth biblical level of the Word is the *two-edged sword*. As stated, the double-edged sword is forged by the voice of God speaking His Word to you and you repeating with your mouth the Word that was spoken. Pocketknives, butter knives, and even meat cleavers will not be effective in strong spiritual warfare; only the long, double-edged sword of the Word of God is prepared for you to use to defend yourself and attack the adversary.

## Two Unnamed Weapons

Years ago while studying the armor of the Roman soldier, comparing it with Ephesians 6, I discovered that there appeared to be two important weapons of the Roman soldier missing from Paul's list in Ephesians 6. The two items were called the *pilum* and the *javelin*. Both were standard pieces of equipment of a fully dressed Roman soldier. The javelin was specifically designed to be thrown and was called a lance.

Paul never mentioned the pilum or javelin by name in his discourse, as perhaps the Roman guards in his cell may not have been carrying these as they were not needed in a prison setting. But they were visible when soldiers were marching or preparing for battle, and these important objects were standard equipment for every Roman soldier. The javelin was long (over six feet), and the pilum was shorter. The longer one was for throwing and the shorter one for gouging the enemy up close. The pilum consisted of a long iron head and a wooden shaft, the long shaft being wood and the upper part being made of iron. Lead weights were placed on the wooden section of the shaft to increase range and impact. In battle, before charging the enemy, the soldier threw his pilum, usually within a distance of twenty to thirty yards. Once it reached its destination and struck the intended object, the metal section would bend from the wooden part, preventing the pilum from being used by the enemy. If the pilum hit the enemy's shield and stuck, it was difficult to pull out, causing the enemy's shield to become cumbersome and difficult to balance. When the battle concluded, the pila were gathered and straightened out in order to be reused in a future battle.[11]

What would these two important weapons on a Roman soldier represent in the life of a believer? Why did Paul somehow omit these two objects in his discourse on the armor of God? I believe Ephesians 6:18 holds part of answer, when Paul wrote:

Praying always with all prayer and supplication in the Spirit, being watchful to this end with all perseverance and supplication for all the saints.

This verse refers to praying with *all types* of prayers. The word *prayer* comes from two words, *pros*, meaning, "face-to-face," and *euche*, meaning, "a desire, vow, or wish." Prayer is a face-to-face meeting with God in order to present to Him your wish or desire. There are various prayers and petitions offered to God at various seasons. There are specific times we are alerted to pray, and we must use various types of prayer. There are times we pray for a healing, then for a miracle, or for financial provision. Certain prayers must be prayed in certain seasons. The Bible refers to "times and seasons" (Acts 1:7; 1 Thess. 5:1). There are two Greek words that identify "time." The first is *chronos*, translated "times" in Acts 1:7. The meaning is a fixed time when something specific is accomplished. The second is *kairos*, translated as "seasons" in Acts 1:7, which alludes to a strategic season of time—a set time of opportunity or a particular appointed time.

Examples of a *kairos* time is when a special window of opportunity is opened (Col. 4:3). It is also a season of sudden temptation (Luke 22:31–32). It can refer to a season of unexpected persecution (Acts 12:1–8). The Greek word is used when Christ spoke of a specific time of harvest when the fruit was ripe (Matt. 13:30). Thus, certain types of prayers are prayed in certain seasons of your life. Prayer is more than communication to God; it is also a weapon of war that releases angelic powers to defeat the stronger principalities of the enemy. (See Daniel 10.) Prayer consists of powerful words that are released into the atmosphere, like a pilum thrust from the hand of the soldier in battle, intended to strike the oncoming enemy and stop his progress.

If the pilum represents *our prayers,* then the second weapon, the javelin or the lance, can represent our *praises,* which not only glorify

God but also are weapons in spiritual battle. I love Psalm 149:6–9, which describes the power of praise to defeat God's enemies:

> Let the high praises of God be in their mouth,
> And a two-edged sword in their hand,
> To execute vengeance on the nations,
> And punishments on the peoples;
> To bind their kings with chains,
> And their nobles with fetters of iron;
> To execute on them the written judgment—
> This honor have all His saints.

The high praises are the exalted words of praise from our hearts to God. The two-edged sword is the Word of God, which is used when engaging in battles. Notice that the spoken *Word* and our *worship* release spiritual authority on earth to bind (put in bonds) enemies and execute the judgments and will of God on the earth. Praise can become a weapon of war!

In 2 Chronicles 20 Scripture reveals the power of singing and worship to defeat Israel's enemies. King Jehoshaphat appointed singers and worshippers to stand upon the mountains, singing and praising God. Suddenly God set ambushes against the enemy, defeating them through the weapon of singing and praise! Thus, the second weapon that is parallel to the Roman javelin is the *praise* that is *shot* up into heaven and brings in return the glory of the Lord in the midst of your conflict. When Paul and Silas were beaten and imprisoned, and their feet placed in wooden stocks, at midnight they began singing and praising God with such volume that the other prisoners heard them. Suddenly the jailhouse began to rock, the result of God striking the prison with an earthquake, cracking the rock foundation and sending the iron prison doors flying off their hinges (Acts 16:22–26). This story illustrates how *praise can rattle your cage*, meaning that worship can bring God's delivering power to where you are and begin melting the bondages (chains) that have you bound. Not only did Paul and Silas benefit from this special midnight praise and worship event, but also, "…immediately all the doors were opened and everyone's chains were loosed" (v. 26). When you worship and your words invite God into your situation, then divine energy fills the atmosphere and can also impact those around you. *A bound person cannot free a bound person; only a free man can deliver a bound man!* Worship invites the Holy Spirit, and "where the Spirit of the Lord is, there is liberty" (2 Cor. 3:17). Praise becomes the *javelin* that confronts the circumstances and the spiritual powers of darkness and brings liberation to you and those around you.

Prayer and worship must become a part of the believer's armor and lifestyle, as these *power twins* of the Christian walk not only express our wishes and worship to God but also create the atmosphere of faith and power to break off chains and smash prison doors that have men and women bound. This body armor is designed to help a believer to stand firm and unmovable in the evil day (Eph. 6:13). Believe me, anyone who has served Christ for a long time will tell you there is an "evil day" planned for you. In the Greek there is a definite article before the word "day," that expositors mark as a specific day, not just a day you are having where things don't go right, but a day that is very evil, wicked, and full of temptation and trials.

The question has been asked, "When Paul spoke of the armor of God, is this armor automatically a part of the believer's daily life, or must we pray that we be covered by the armor of God?" I believe the best way to answer this question is to relate a story that was told to me by a dear pastor friend in Texas, who was close friends with the minister and his family to whom this astonishing event happened.

Several years ago one of the outstanding spiritual leaders in the charismatic movement and in the body of Christ pastored a large, growing church in Texas. The pastor had several children, including a daughter who worked in the office and handled the mail and packages coming into the church. The pastor had taught his children about the armor of God and the importance, before going to work each morning, of confessing with their mouths that their minds were covered by the helmet of salvation, their hearts were protected by the shield of faith, and their feet were prepared to carry the gospel. Basically, every part of the armor listed in Ephesians 6 was applied by faith and confessing the Word.

On one particular morning the daughter was running a little late and almost forgot to review her daily confession concerning the armor of God. She felt there was a need to do so, and she took the time to speak the normal pattern. She also was impressed to wear a leather-type dress to work. She had no clue why, but she was certain she was supposed to wear this particular outfit.

When she arrived, she was sitting at her desk opening the mail and began to open a package. Suddenly there was a loud explosion, and the package blew up in her lap. It was a pipe bomb, and its force was powerful enough to blow off the wooden arms of the chair on which she sat. Because she wore the leather dress, the nails and metal from the explosion actually stuck into the leather, and she survived a very deadly situation.[12]

This true store was related to me many years ago, and each time I read the weapons in the armor list, I am reminded of this amazing protective event. In reality, many of the spiritual blessings in the Bible become realities in our spiritual and daily lives through the means of confession. Salvation is manifested when, "With the heart one believes unto righteousness, and with the mouth confession is made unto salvation" (Rom. 10:10). This God gear is invisible to the natural eye, yet it is activated through our knowledge of the Word and our faith and trust in God's promises.

You may not see the armor with your natural eyes, just as Job did not see a "hedge" around him with his natural eyes (Job 1:10), but the adversary knows if you are fully clothed or partially naked, and he knows if you truly believe or if you are going to "fake it till you make it." The Bible teaches that we overcome Satan by the "blood of the Lamb" (Rev. 12:11). Christ's blood was shed in AD 32, and we cannot visibly see the blood applied to our spirits when we ask for forgiveness of sins. However, God and Christ sit in heaven, and through faith we recall the defeat of Satan, which was accomplished by Christ's death and His suffering; thus the invisible is made visible and Satan's past defeat becomes a repeated present reality.

As a soldier, you would never go to war without proper training, weapons, and protective gear. The Bible is our training guide; our life experiences and spiritual walk become our boot camp; and the temptations, trials, and attacks we face are all a part of the warfare. As a Christian engaged in spiritual conflicts, you must never leave home without your mind and heart covered and fully clothed with the warfare gear. Paul said, "Put on the whole armor" (Eph. 6:11). The armor of God—never leave home without it!

# Chapter 2

# INHERITING YOUR
# ANCESTORS' DEMONS

G OD THINKS AND PLANS IN A GENERATIONAL MANNER, keeping His promises for a thousand generations (Ps. 105:8). Divine favor and covenant promises can be transferred from father to son. Take the example of our spiritual father Abraham. The Almighty made a covenant with Abraham, promising him a son and a future nation (Gen. 15:4–7). At age one hundred, Abraham saw his son Isaac born through his ninety-year-old wife, Sarah. Isaac's wife conceived twins (Jacob and Esau), and Jacob later fathered twelve sons, who themselves became identified as the fathers of the twelve tribes of Israel. When Jacob went to Egypt as an older patriarch, there were "seventy souls" that came from him (Exod. 1:5, KJV). However, four hundred years later, six hundred thousand men of war departed with their wives and children from Egypt (Exod. 12:37). If the future sons of Abraham followed the footsteps of their father and ancestor, obeying the commands of the Lord, they would inherit the spiritual and natural blessings flowing from the Lord that were promised to Abraham. The same is true, however, when evil men pass on their evil inclinations into the bloodline of their future sons.

## The Terrorists of Gadara

Travel back in time with me to the lower Galilee, where on the eastern mountains surrounding the famous Sea of Galilee a small city called Gadara existed—part of ten Hellenized cities called the Decapolis—and it was buzzing with activity. These cities were dominated with Greek culture, including pagan temples built in which to worship idols. In that time when an inhabitant of the cities died, his body was wrapped in linen and the corpse slid into a long niche carved inside a large limestone cavern called a *sepulture*. In the narrative in Mark 5, these carved chambers in rock were called "tombs" (Mark 5:2). After the physical body deteriorated (about one year after burial), the bones were washed and permanently placed in a small stone-carved box called an *ossuary*, and the new box of bones received permanent residence in one of the many niches in the whitewashed limestone sepultures.

In Mark 5 an unnamed man was living among the graves of the dead and was terrorizing the community. His cries were heard night and day; some attempted to bind him with chains and fetters, and he would break them. Eventually Jesus came to town and cast the evil spirits out of the man. There were so many evil spirits that they called themselves "Legion," a word that described as many as six thousand Roman foot soldiers. When the man encountered Christ, He expelled two thousand individual demons from the man's body, and the evil spirits entered into a herd of two thousand swine (v. 13). It is believed these swine were actually being raised by the locals to feed the countless Roman soldiers in that area (as devout Jews did not and do not eat pork). During a Holy Land tour one of my Jewish guides noted that among the Greeks, the god Zeus was worshipped, and there were temples in Christ's time built in honor of Zeus. The priest of Zeus offered swine on the altar. Perhaps these unclean animals were also used as offerings to Zeus in the area of the Decapolis. If so, then through the deliverance of one demon-possessed man Christ eliminated the sacrifices to be offered to the false god of the Greeks!

When the chief demon spoke through the man, he presented a strange offer to Christ:

> For He said to him, "Come out of the man, unclean spirit!" Then He asked him, "What is your name?" And he answered, saying, "My name is Legion; for we are many." Also he begged Him earnestly that He would not send them out of the country.
>
> —MARK 5:8–10

Christ revealed to His disciples what occurs after the unclean spirit is expelled from a person. The unclean spirit goes into dry places seeking rest and cannot find it, and then he seeks to return to the place and person from which he was forced to depart (Luke 11:24). Thus, evil and unclean spirits desire to remain in the regions where they are familiar and dwell in that territory in an attempt to repossess its victim at a later time, bringing seven more wicked spirits with him (vv. 24–26). This could be one explanation as to how a particular spirit that controlled your ancestor could actually remain in the house or the family lineage for several generations, until it is exposed and expelled through the power of Christ's redemptive covenant.

Before you believe this is not possible, consider three things from the story that this unclean spirit did not want.

- - - - - - - - - - - - - - - - - - - - - - - - - - - - - - - - - - - - - -

## Three Demonic Requests

1. The *presence of Christ* tormented the spirits. The main spirit spoke to Christ through the man and asked, "Have

You come here to torment us before the time?" (Matt. 8:29). The living, thriving, presence of the light of Christ always clashes with the darkness of evil. Demonic spirits are totally uncomfortable in the presence of Christ, and this includes a flowing anointing and vibrant worship that is operating in a local church.

2. The chief demon already knew his future destiny and requested Christ *not send him into the abyss*, or the bottomless pit—the final prison of all of Satan's evil team (Luke 8:31; Eph. 6:12; Rev. 9:1–11). This indicates that the inhabitants of the kingdom of darkness already know their final destination and do not want to be sent into confinement before the appointed time.

3. The third and most important point in this study is that spirits dwelling in a particular city or region are *familiar with that region* and desire to remain in the *comfort zone* of their familiarity.

-----------------------------------------------------

It must be made clear here that the subject of inheriting your ancestors' *spirits* has nothing to do with what is called *ancestral spirit worship* among some Asian religions. There are major world religions that believe a human has at least two parts (a physical body and spirit body). The human spirit is freed at death and the body returns to the earth. This is actually a biblical concept, as man came from dust and shall return to dust, and to be absent from the body is to be present (your spirit present) with the Lord (Gen. 3:19; 2 Cor. 5:6). However, in some Asian countries the living consider these departed human spirits as roaming and hovering around their families endlessly. In some cultures chairs are set out during special meals for the *ancestor spirit*. In some European cultures, however, the spirits of a departed person (called *ghosts*) are considered dangerous, and it is believed they can retaliate against the living.

Among some Native American Indians shamans use spirit guides, which they teach are the spirits of the dead, to make contact with the living. In what is called the New Age movement, many New Age gurus and other mediums attempt to channel the spirits of the dead in order to gain secret information. These *higher spirits*, called the *ascended masters*, are allegedly the most desirable to make contact with. From both the Old and New Testaments it is clear that attempting to consult the dead to reveal the future is forbidden and was a weird custom among the early heathen nations (Deut. 18:9–12). The New Testament is clear that when a sinner or a believer passes from this life, there are two specific and opposite locations where the souls and spirits travel and remain until the resurrection and the final judgment. The sinner is carried into a lower chamber in the earth called hell (Luke 16:23), and the believer is taken to the third heaven to paradise (2 Cor. 12:1–4). Any form of ancestor spirit that would appear and receive worship is a *seducing spirit* (1 Tim. 4:1), or a *spirit of deception,* and is considered a manifestation of a familiar spirit (Lev. 20:27; 1 Sam. 28).

One of the most bizarre stories illustrating how a familiar spirit remains in a specific region was related to me by my father, Fred Stone. On this day in the early 1950s Dad was watching several of the smaller children of his family at the family home. Later in the day he began to hear voices coming from a room that was on the side (like an attic), which always remained locked. As the voices became louder, profanity, including cursing God's name, came from the room. The voice sounded like his granddad Stone, and my dad thought Granddad had become drunk with another fellow and had gone to the room and was still under the influence. Dad finally rebuked them out loud from where he was standing (outside the door) in the name of Jesus. Suddenly the voices were silent.

Shortly thereafter family members returned to the house, and Dad told them of the two drunken men in the side room and how Granddad Stone needed to be rebuked for his language. One of Dad's sisters replied, "Fred, Granddad is not here; he went to Bandy, Virginia, early this morning." This sister went to get a key to unlock the door, and when they entered the room, there were no people in the room; this was the only entrance or exit to the room. After realizing these were evil spirits, Dad began to ponder *why* or how these spirits would gain access to that particular room. He then recalled something that had been preserved in that room for many years.

Dad's mother, Nalvie, years ago had previously been married to her first husband, a man named Arthur Ball. One morning Arthur went hunting and never returned home. When a team of men went searching for him, they discovered his body near a fallen tree, where he had tripped and the shotgun had accidentally fired, removing a portion of his face. Evidence of blood on his fingers and parts of his face showed he had lived and even struggled for a brief time. Arthur was buried, but for some reason his blood-covered shirt was taken to the attic room and stored there by Nalvie for many years. Dad believed that the only thing in the attic that would attract these spirits was the blood-covered shirt. Remember that some false religions offer blood of animals to draw spirits to them or in hopes of inducing a curse upon someone.

Before a person writes this idea off as a fantasy or an overactive imagination, remember that certain things attract spirits. In the Bible God was against any and all forms of idolatry, as idol and false god worship was considered the worship of devils (1 Cor. 10:19–21; Rev. 9:20). In nations where temples are built to idol gods, there is always a massive operation and manifestation of demonic spirits, possessing the worshippers and bringing with them sickness, oppression, fear, and superstition. Any nation that worships man-made idols will be infested with all forms of evil, unclean, foul, and familiar spirits.

There are certain religions such as voodoo, an ancient West African religious practice followed by millions in Africa and by many in the Caribbean Islands, such as Haiti, that involves demonic activity. The original name is *vodou* and means, "spirit." Because Haiti is a poor nation, the blood of a chicken or birds is used to perform ritual curses and stir up the spirits, or it's offered as a sacrifice to some strange god.

The practice of voodoo came to Haiti during the 1700s when many Africans were being seized as slaves and were transported to Haiti and other Caribbean islands. In 1791 a powerful witch doctor named Boukman led a rebellion of a hundred of slaves who revolted against the French and vowed to die for liberty. On August 14, 1791, these slaves held a voodoo ceremony pledging allegiance to their voodoo spirits in return for liberty. This ceremony, known as the Bwa Kayiman ceremony, came to be known as *the pact with the devil*. According to many sources, this covenant with darkness is renewed yearly on August 14. The practice of voodoo has been prominent in Haiti since this time in 1791.[1]

In 1957 a man named Francois Duvalier, also called "Papa Doc," became the dictator of Haiti. He was very steeped in voodoo, and the story among the Haitians is that this man sold his soul to the devil, using not just the blood of animals but also human blood from infants and virgins in his voodoo rituals. He cast his spell over the Haitian people through his artful use of voodoo, ruling in a reign of terror for fourteen years.[2]

Haiti's government has officially sanctioned voodoo as a religion and allows practitioners to perform ceremonies, including baptisms, marriages, and others. It has been reported that almost every family in Haiti has someone who practices voodoo—serves the spirits, who holds the "traditional beliefs."[3]

It should be pointed out that Haiti is considered the poorest country in the Western Hemisphere, as poverty always follows the worship of false gods or idols.

Years ago I ministered in a Mississippi church in which the pastor was a former missionary leader in Haiti for a major denomination. He was in Haiti when President Kennedy announced the blockade against Cuba (with other countries inside the blockade zone, including Haiti), and he related to me a story that was known at that time among the voodoo high priests. He said that "Papa Doc" called into his palace the most powerful voodoo priests, instructing them to create a voodoo doll to represent President Kennedy. During the actual ritual large pins were placed into the back of the head of the doll, placing incantations and curses upon the American president and requesting a powerful spirit to be released against him and for someone to be found to kill Kennedy. Having survived six assassination attempts on his own life, Papa Doc was very superstitious and would only go out in public on the twenty-second of each month, with the belief he was being protected by certain spirits from death. It was an odd "coincidence" that President Kennedy was shot in the back of the head by an assassin on the twenty-second day of November.[4]

It should be pointed out that the occult world does operate under various levels of demonic influence, and any person who is not in a true covenant with God and is walking in unrighteousness does not enjoy the invisible protective hedge to prevent demonic spirits from engaging in unwanted activity in his or her life. Curses only work upon those who have no protective hedge or upon individuals who place confidence in the power of the curse.

## The Spirit Attacking Our Genealogy

I paid little attention to this when growing up, but in my teens I began seeing a manifestation of a family trait that emerged on my father's side of the family. From childhood to my mid-teen years

I was a rather happy-go-lucky, hardworking young man who was self-motivated. To bring in personal income, I cut grass, became janitor of the church where Dad pastored, and cleaned people's cars at the apartments across the street from our house in Salem, Virginia. The Holy Spirit called me into the ministry at age sixteen; after hours of prayer on a Sunday night, I announced to my three friends praying with me that God had called me to preach. Everything went normal until I began full-time evangelistic ministry at age eighteen.

From that time forward it seemed I lived under a heavy cloud of mental oppression and depression. For several years there was not a day in which I did not feel some form of negative pressure on my mind, making my entire body feel like a dead weight was pressing my spirit down. Only after long hours of prayer each day was there any relief. I realized some of this pressure was a spiritual burden for the lost and the desire to see spiritual results at the altar, and it was part of the price to pay to break through the enemy's strongholds in a town and city. Eventually I discovered that every town and city had its own spiritual atmosphere, and it was necessary for me to mentally and spiritually adjust to each particular setting and learn how to pierce the darkness through the spear of prayer and the weapon of fasting.

After several years of battling depression (something only my closest friends were aware of), I began studying familiar spirits and how spirits desire to remain in the region where they have dwelt or among the families of whom they are familiar (Mark 5:9–10). I knew that my father's mom had experienced a major nervous breakdown many years ago. Grandma Stone was the sweetest and most gentle woman you can imagine. However, as a child I remember seeing her lay on one side on the couch or bed and talk to herself as she tore small pieces of paper up and placed them in a red bowl—a bowl that was used to spit tobacco juice in. She could carry on a normal conversation and was very loving to everyone, but the breakdown did have a long-term effect on her in different ways. Dad had a sister who also experienced an emotional breakdown. My wife's own precious mother had experienced a similar emotional collapse when she was about thirty years of age and Pam was only fourteen years of age. My dad's own father, William Stone, broke under mental pressure, and he too experienced a breakdown in the 1970s. Several years after I was married on April 2, 1982, at a time when I was sharing about these seasons of depression with my wife, the *light* came on! It appears I was dealing with some type of a familiar spirit—not one possessing me but one oppressing me, hoping to work its power against me, wearing me down mentally to a breaking point as it had different family members in the past.

This oppression, which had continued for about five years, finally broke soon after I recognized this oppression from a familiar spirit, and as a benefit of my marriage to my wife, Pam. I observed that the oppression, depression, and anxiety I had experienced were replaced with peace and joy. The marriage to my sweetheart had filled a void spot of loneliness. A passage written by Solomon helped explain this:

> Two are better than one,
> Because they have a good reward for their labor.
> For if they fall, one will lift up his companion.
> But woe to him who is alone when he falls,
> For he has no one to help him up.
> Again, if two lie down together, they will keep warm;
> But how can one be warm alone?
> —ECCLESIASTES 4:9–11

A single person should marry in God's will and not to avoid loneliness or escape from your parents, or because of some raging hormones. It should be out of mutual love and agreement of being in God's will. However, there is an increase in *spiritual authority* when two are join together. It only requires two to be in agreement, asking in faith, "concerning anything that they ask, [and] it will be done for them" (Matt. 18:19). With Pam by my side, two were now praying for the revivals, two were agreeing for the ministry, two were walking in faith, and two increases spiritual authority over the enemy. There was also the amazing power of love to soothe fear and anxiety. In conferences I often encounter people battling fear, who request for me to pray that the "spirit of fear" (2 Tim. 1:7) depart from them. I remind them of this verse:

> There is no fear in love; but perfect love casts out fear, because fear involves torment. But he who fears has not been made perfect in love.
>
> —1 JOHN 4:18

Every believer should have a godly fear, but *not* a fear of Satan, of men, or of the future. The Greek word for "torment" is *kolosis*; it refers to "correction, punishment, and penalty" and brings with it the idea of some form of punishment. All fear plants seeds of the idea of something bad happening, or of a penalty or retaliation. When we understand the full level of God's love—that He is *for us* and not against us, *with us* and not distant from us, *in us* and not rejecting us—then fear of spiritual or eternal correction or penalty (loss of reward) at the judgment seat of Christ is diminished. If God is for us, then who can be against us?[5]

The emotion and expressions of love that bonds two people release certain *feel-good* chemicals within the body, which bring a sense of serenity and peace to the receiver. These feel-good chemicals, such as dopamine, serotonin, and endorphins, are released through hugs, kisses, and holding hands. These feel-good moments also build upon the feelings of trust, bonding, and confidence, forging a strong emotion and belief that you and your companion can conquer the world and defeat any adversity. Notice that perfect love "casts out," or "throws off and removes," fear.

Having met and ministered to tens of thousands of individuals, I have observed that those struggling with fear of their past and spirits that have attacked their family often speak of numerous broken relationships, family strife, and contention in the home. Division breaks the *love factor* and weakens God's ultimate weapon to defeat any spirit. When you love God with all of your soul, mind, and spirit along with your companion, family, and fellow believers (let's not forget the sinners), you are filling your heart and love tank with so much love that fear has no room to dwell.

My battle with depression and doubt was caused by a spirit at work that had attacked previous family members for several generations. One of the greatest freedom-discovering truths was when I realized Jesus loves me, He wanted me free, and He was the same Christ who could deliver me today, just as He did in the Bible times (Heb. 13:8).

## DELIVERANCE FROM ANCESTRAL DEMONS

If you are concerned about spirits from your past lineage being passed down to the next generation, you should first examine the moral or spiritual weaknesses in your family tree. For example, Cain slew Abel his brother, and in Cain's lineage a descendant named Lamech also killed a man (Gen. 4:23–24). Among the early patriarchs, Abraham lied and said that Sarah was his sister (this was partially true—Sarah was the daughter of Abraham's father but had a different mother), but he did so out of fear (Gen. 12:13). Isaac also fibbed about his wife being his sister out of fear (Gen. 26:7), and Jacob was deceived by his eleven sons, who conspired secretly, saying Joseph was slain by a wild beast when he had been sold as a servant (Gen. 37).

The lineage of David appears to have struggled with the opposite sex. David committed adultery and later discovered that his son had raped a half-sister (2 Sam. 13). Solomon, the son who replaced David as king, was addicted to strange women and married seven hundred wives plus three hundred concubines (1 Kings 11:3). When looking at your lineage, does a particular sickness, divorce, adultery, or some other moral or spiritual weakness such as fear or depression pass on from generation to generation? While some physical ailments can be DNA acquired, most *moral disruptions* can be the adversary, playing on a weakness like a hidden earthquake's fault line running through the family, which can rupture at any moment.

There is a Christian family who has several grown children, all now having their own children. The mother divorced the father many years ago and remained aloof from her own children for several years, "starting her own new life." There were several obvious weaknesses in the mother that were blatant and known to all who knew her. Eventually the mother passed away. However, after her mother's passing, one of her daughters began to take on the traits, attitudes, and manner of thinking she had never had before—all of which were the same negative traits her mother had lived with. It is quite possible that upon the mother's death, the spirit that had controlled her life was now passed to a child in her lineage who somehow became open to the voice of motivation of that spirit. The change in the woman was too obvious to be ignored. *Spirits can only be expelled when they have been exposed!*

You must also clean your dwelling place—house, apartment, or college dorm—of anything that would attract a spirit or open the door for demonic activity. In my book *Purging Your House, Pruning Your Family Tree* I list six specific things that can attract spirits to your home:[6]

1. Pornography

2. Occult games

3. Illegal drugs

4. Alcohol and strong drinks

5. Sexual perversion

6. Physic hotlines and occult activities

In the time of the apostles the availability of certain sins was not as accessible as it is today. The first-century population had no computers and instant Internet, no phones that can view videos and so forth. However, as recorded in Acts, once believers entered the new covenant, if they had in their possession any items that were idols or used in the occult, these items were collected and burned. We read that during a great revival in the city of Ephesus:

> Also, many of those who had practiced magic brought their books together and burned them in the sight of all. And they counted up the value of them, and it totaled fifty thousand pieces of silver.
>
> —ACTS 19:19

If there are idols, occult books or games, pornography, illegal drugs, or other abusive substances in your possession, they must be removed from your premises, as these things are like dung that attracts flies. These feed the mind, body, and spirit of a person the wrong "food," and mental images and the wrong food will clog the arteries to the heart and in the brain—both natural food (too much fat) and the wrong spiritual food (too much junk). Soon your heart weakens and your mind ceases to reason properly and resist evil. Fainting in your spirit soon follows, and you find yourself in a life-and-death struggle.

Third, you must understand the protective power and authority you have in the new covenant under Christ. No matter what sin, spirit, or weakness your family has battled, the new covenant and learning the Word of God create in you a renewed mind, a clean heart, and right thinking, making you a new creation. We read:

> Therefore, if anyone is in Christ, he is a new creation; old things have passed away; behold, all things have become new.
> —2 CORINTHIANS 5:17

There are powerful promises and revelations that reveal how Christ has defeated Satan and his rebels through His death and resurrection. This would include any type of spirit that was part of your ancestral lineage. John wrote:

> He who sins is of the devil, for the devil has sinned from the beginning. For this purpose the Son of God was manifested, that He might destroy the works of the devil.
> —1 JOHN 3:8

Christ did not destroy the devil, as the person of the devil—the fallen angel—still exists and is quite active on earth. Christ did, however, destroy the *works* of the adversary. The word *destroy* is used thirty-two times in the King James translation of the Bible. The common Greek word for "destroy" is *apollumi* and can refer to "fully destroying, to lose, to perish or destroy." Here, however, John used the Greek word *luoto*, which means, "to dissolve, to melt, or to loosen." An example of the same word and concept is found in Matthew 16:19:

> And I will give you the keys of the kingdom of heaven, and whatever you bind on earth will be bound in heaven, and whatever you loose on earth will be loosed in heaven.

## LOOSED FROM THE ENEMY'S HOLD

The Greek word for "loose" here is *luo* and refers to "loose, unbind and to release." It includes loosing shoes (Mark 1:7), of animals

(Matt. 21:2), and of persons (John 11:44). To loose something in Matthew 16:19 was to undo on earth what had been undone in heaven. The idea of spiritually binding and loosing is understood in Mark 7:35, where Jesus "loosed" the tongue of a person who was unable to speak, curing the man and enabling him to speak for the first time in his life. Also, in Luke 13:12 Christ prayed for a woman with a spirit of infirmity and commanded, "Woman, you are loosed from your infirmity." The spirit of weakness immediately departed when Christ released the woman from her eighteen-year-long sickness. God's will in heaven was to undo the sin, sickness, and infirmity placed upon humanity. God's servants on earth are to act upon their delegated spiritual authority and release those on earth who are bound by sin and eternal death, and to take authority over all the power of the enemy!

Greek scholar Tony Scott said that the word *loose* has the original meaning of two boards that were glued together and the glue was bad, thus the two boards "come unglued" or they "lose consistency."[7] Using this imagery, the adversary has some people glued to a hard bondage, an addiction, or a lifestyle of sin. The power of the blood of Christ, the name of Jesus, and the Word of God will undo the glue of the bondage to which a person is stuck! There's no "glue" so strong that the grip of God cannot break it loose!

In John 8:36 we read, "Therefore if the Son makes you free, you shall be free indeed." The Greek word for "free" means not only "to liberate" but also "to exempt from liability." The word in Roman times referred to a free person who was a citizen and not a slave. The liability here refers to the penalty for a life of sin and for being a slave to Satan and disobedience, but the new freedom that Christ brings releases the individual from the penalty and power of sin. In the New Testament the idea of freedom is that of a slave being released (redeemed, purchased) out of the slave market and then given his or her personal freedom.

There has never been a time since the resurrection of Christ that any satanic power, familiar spirit, or any demonic spirit could prevent the act of redemption and salvation from occurring when any person from any part of the world submitted himself or herself to Christ and asked Him for redemption through His blood (Col. 1:4). This is why Paul wrote:

> For I am persuaded that neither death nor life, nor angels nor principalities nor powers, nor things present nor things to come, nor height nor depth, nor any other created thing, shall be able to separate us from the love of God which is in Christ Jesus our Lord.
> —ROMANS 8:38–39

Your first action must be to determine if what you are experiencing is being initiated or agitated by a spirit. If so, there will often be a terrible, cold, and dark presence that can be felt consistently in the home or the dwelling place, as evil spirits create a sense of dread, depression, and fear. I have suggested for families to take anointing oil and walk through every room, dedicating the house and each room to Christ and anointing the posts of the door and speaking blessing, favor, and God's protection over the house.

I have also on numerous occasions used a method of "confessing the blood of Christ" over hotel rooms where I have stayed during conferences. Many different types of individuals travel and use hotel lodgings, and you are unaware of who has been sleeping in the bed prior to your arrival. On one occasion in West Virginia, for three nights in a row I was awakened by some type of spirit pulling the cover off, shaking the bed, and even pressing up against my back. All three times when I rebuked it, the invisible entity departed. However, I finally stood in the room and confessed in faith that Christ's blood and His Word was my hedge when I was in the room, and no spirit that was not of God was permitted in the room from that point on. In each case this method of *resisting* and *rebuking* spirits was successful. Each time when this has occurred, I am reminded of the promises in Revelation 12:11: "And they overcame him by the blood of the Lamb and by the word of their testimony."

To maintain a victorious life, refuse to think or act in the manner that your unconverted family members did that opened the door to spiritual powers and family conflicts. If you struggle with a hot temper, quit excusing it by saying, "You know Dad had a violent temper, so I get it from him!" If you battle depression, put a stop to justifying its grip by saying, "All the women on Mom's side of the family suffer depression." If your dad and granddad loved pornography, don't give the enemy any place by saying, "It's just a weakness that runs in the family, and all of us men have it!" *Remember, you will never change what you permit, and never challenge what you allow.* There is power in the blood of Christ, the name of Christ, and in His authority to loose you from the influence of any type of spirit. Ask and pray in faith. This promise is for all who need freedom from satanic opposition:

> Therefore submit to God. Resist the devil and he will flee
> from you. Draw near to God and He will draw near to you.
> —JAMES 4:7–8

The word *submit* here is an old English word meaning, "to be subject to," and refers to a lesser one submitting to a greater one. The verb means, "to place or arrange under." The word *resist* means, "to array against," and the implication is that if you will place yourself under God's instruction, direction, and protection, placing yourself under His authority, then you will be able to resist and withstand (stand against) any assault of the enemy.[8] This includes defeating and expelling any spirit—past, present, or future—as Christ has. "All authority...in heaven and on earth"

(Matt. 28:18). All spirits are subject unto Him. We as believers have been given His authority over all the powers of the enemy, and nothing shall hurt us if we are walking and abiding in that authority (Luke 10:19).

# *Chapter 3*

# WINNING IN PUBLIC—
# LOSING IN PRIVATE

N O ONE KNEW HE WAS BATTLING THE SPIRIT OF DEPRES-
sion and hopelessness. He was known as a great pastor, a
well-known minister of the gospel, pastoring a large church where
the members respected him and his wife and two sons. There was
nothing in particular going on that would cause him to hit a pit of
despair and eventually be found dead, where all evidence indicated
he took his own life. Questions were posed with no answers. Was
there something hidden that others did not know that was overwhelming to him? *His victorious preaching gave no sign of a private
struggle.*

As a redeemed, church-attending, tithe-paying, faithful believer,
it is possible that your closest friends and family have not heard
*all of your testimony*, as you "pick and choose" the stories you want
people to know and avoid what you are trying to forget! Some
believers do have *skeletons in their closet* and pray the doors of their
past remain closed and lock. Some women who are now mothers

have been sacrificed on the altar of silence to protect an older member of the family who abused her as a child. The person you see smiling in church on Sunday morning and testifying to a public victory may return home and be fighting private struggles that are paving a road to a dead-end private defeat.

It is quite challenging for any believer who is living by the guidelines of Scripture and seeking to be holy and in right standing before God to admit he or she is struggling with a private bondage, addiction, or fleshly lust. It is not always pride that prevents a confession, but fear of the reaction of others to the confession. If you were to admit to a spiritual or emotional battle, would you totally trust the ears of the person(s) hearing your confession? Information swirling in the mind can easily be released through loose lips, and important information—especially secret facts—holds certain power with those who know the *whole story*. A husband may hesitate to confess his infidelity or mental temptations to his companion for fear he will not be forgiven or that his wife may take a permanent walk, passing by the divorce court on the way back to Momma's house. The public smile is a cover for the pain in the soul that needs healing, but fear locks the door and keeps a tormented soul chained in a mental prison of condemnation. With addictions, there is the fear that exposing the bondage would lead to rehab and only bring a temporary relief, as the addict would eventually return to the same mire from which he or she was pulled.

## THE WINNER IS...

In the Bible no one won more *public victories* in war than David. He was the youngest of eight sons of Jesse (1 Sam. 16:11; 17:14), yet he stood face-to-face with a Philistine giant, defeating him and instantly winning the hearts of the nation. From that moment David was assigned as Saul's armor bearer, warring against the Philistines and protecting the king from threats. However, on one occasion David became discouraged, and in an unwise act he traveled to Gath, Goliath's home town, with Goliath's sword, almost in an arrogant manner. He was briefly arrested, faked insanity in front of the king, and was later released (1 Sam. 21:10–22:1). At age thirty David became king and served God for many years, building the tabernacle of David on Mount Zion, a center for continual worship to God. (See 1 Chronicles 15–16.)

At the peak of David's kingly career he became complacent, overly confident, and too comfortable as his manly instinct to conquer was turned away from conquering enemies to conquering a woman. It appears he was at midlife, and instead of going to battle with his men, David was lying around the palace sleeping in late. We read:

> It happened in the spring of the year, at the time when kings go out to battle, that David sent Joab and his servants with him, and all Israel; and they destroyed the people of Ammon and besieged Rabbah. But David remained at Jerusalem. Then it happened one evening that David arose from his bed and walked on the roof of the king's house. And from the roof he saw a woman bathing, and the woman was very beautiful to behold. So David sent and inquired about the woman. And someone said, "Is this not Bathsheba, the daughter of Eliam, the wife of Uriah the Hittite?" Then David sent messengers, and took her; and she came to him, and he lay with her, for she was cleansed from her impurity; and she returned to her house. And the woman conceived; so she sent and told David, and said, "I am with child."
>
> —2 Samuel 11:1–5

## The Progression of a Private Fall

There are five significant points to be made with David that reveal the progression of a private moral failure.

THE WRONG PLACE

The text indicates that it was a time of war, when kings were at battle, but David, Israel's king, sent his men to fight *for* him; he was not fighting *with* them. His place was the battlefield, but he was in the palace. David was in the *wrong place*.

THE WRONG TIME

The second clue to the mystery of the private struggle was David arose at "eveningtide" (v. 2, KJV). The word *eveningtide* indicates the king was sleeping in very late, as the word alludes to sometime late in the afternoon. He should have awakened early, as he indicated in the Psalms that "early" he would seek the Lord (Ps. 63:1). Thus David was in the wrong place at the *wrong time*.

THE WRONG SETTING

The third point is a deduction from the story. David was married to Saul's daughter, positioning her as the queen of the kingdom. However, when David brought the *girlfriend* into their bedroom, David's wife, Michal, is missing from the story. Thus, David's men are at war and his wife is absent from the palace (or doesn't care about his indiscretion), making this a threefold cord of wrong place, wrong time, and *wrong setting*!

THE WRONG THOUGHTS

In that day the city of David was constructed on the hill of Mount Zion, and the king's palace sat above the homes of the people. The roofs were flat, and when David stood on his balcony, he saw a woman bathing herself. This makes Bathsheba seem as though she is seeking attention to bathe in such a public setting. However there is a key phrase: "she was purified from her uncleanness" (2 Sam. 11:4, KJV). This would indicate the reason for bathing. When a woman was experiencing her monthly menstrual cycle, she was ceremonially unclean. Once her cycle had concluded, she bathed herself to be purified from her uncleanness. Since the men were at war and the king should have been at battle, then Bathsheba's bath on the roof (where rainwater was collected in barrels) was not an act of seduction. Her motive was for cleansing, but David's motive was self-serving. As David observed her, the fourth point becomes obvious; David's mind has begun to think the *wrong thoughts*.

## THE WRONG ACTIONS

The fifth point is that after inquiring who she was (another man's wife), instead of saying, "Just wondering," he said, "Bring her to my bedroom." Thus the fivefold downward path from life to spiritual death—wrong place, wrong time, wrong setting, and wrong thought, which led to *wrong actions*. David's fivefold pattern for decline reveals that his failure was not a sudden, overwhelming urge that he could not resist, but it was well orchestrated for his personal pleasure.

## THE ROOTS OF FAILURE

For many years I was puzzled as to how a man after God's own heart (1 Sam 13:14) and a godly king would allow himself to fall so low into such a trap of adultery, conspiracy, and murder. Perhaps David assumed that with Bathsheba's husband (Uriah) out of town, he would never discover their indiscretion. With the men of Israel at war, few people would ever see the secret entry into the palace, and neither he nor she thought she would end up pregnant. Thus, David thought that he and Bathsheba would sneak into the palace, in the bed, out of the bed, out of the palace, and back home without any observation. However, the real question becomes not *how* the plan was set up but *what motivated* the setup to begin with. The easier explanation is that David fell into a burning lust, and

Bathsheba willingly submitted. However, behind every major spiritual calamity is a hidden *root* buried underneath the rubble.

Consider the condition of David's marriage. He was wed to Michal, the daughter of King Saul, who gave her to David to be a snare to him:

> So Saul said, "I will give her to him, that she may be a snare to him, and that the hand of the Philistines may be against him." Therefore Saul said to David a second time, "You shall be my son-in-law today."
>
> —1 SAMUEL 18:21

David's wife, Michal, had her father's DNA, as illustrated when David brought the ark of the covenant to Jerusalem with dancing and singing. Michal's response was to rebuke David for his expressive worship and to mock him in her heart (1 Chron. 15:29). Since David was a worshipper from his youth, his wife's criticism of his worship cut into his spirit, and in return he cut her off from the physical marital bed, as she "had no children to the day of her death" (2 Sam. 6:23). From the moment she mocked him, she is not mentioned in the narrative of David's life again. Thus, David's marriage was not just in serious condition, but for all practical purposes it was dead.

Now consider Bathsheba's husband, Uriah. Few casual readers of Scripture know that Uriah was an important soldier in David's army and listed as one of David's "mighty men." In 2 Samuel 23 there is a detailed list of men who surrounded David and became his personal army. The total number was six hundred, but among the six hundred there were thirty-seven who were more superior than others in the group. Uriah the Hittite was listed as one of the thirty-seven (v. 39). This same Uriah was the husband of Bathsheba (2 Sam. 11:3). After David discovered Bathsheba was pregnant with his child, he called Uriah from the front line, inviting him for a two-day break from the battle to spend time at home with his wife. Uriah refused, sleeping on the palace steps—*the same steps his wife walked up to secretly meet David*—refusing to go home. Uriah reminded the king that the warriors of Israel were dwelling in tents, and he could not enjoy the comfort of home while the men sacrificed on the battlefield (v. 11). Twice David offered Uriah time at home, and twice he refused (vv. 7–13).

Uriah's dedication to the army was commendable. However, his actions reveal an important point. Most men with a beautiful wife would rejoice at the opportunity to break away from the battle and spend some quality time with their companion. Uriah is an example of a man totally dedicated to his work, and one who today could be identified as a workaholic. If Uriah was caught up in his own work, business, or the battles, then Bathsheba may have been the wife starving for attention from an overachieving husband.

THE ROOT OF EMOTIONAL NEED

Christian counselors who deal with extramarital affairs say that it is common for a woman to be attracted to a man in power or position, as this represents security, one of the most important needs in a woman's life. It often has nothing to do with looks or age, as the idea of a powerful man interested in her who will give her the attention she is craving feeds her ego like a drug. The man with a bad marriage who has a wife who is nagging, criticizing, or mocking him, or one who shows no affection, can become susceptible to or attracted to a woman who will brag on him, especially if she is physically attractive.

Some suggest that David had no *affection* and Bathsheba had no *attention*, and when these two needs cross paths, it is an invitation to trouble. As the roots of a lack of attention and affection grow, they can push a couple apart and bring forth fruit of emotional separation long before physical separation. There may have, however, been a much greater root that birthed the tree of sin and the fruit of unrighteousness in David's life.

## THE ROOT OF COMFORT

The second root is simple and often secretly grows in the hearts of successful individuals. As long as David was on the run from Saul, his total dependency was upon God's supernatural defense and protection. Once David became king of Israel, his success, prosperity, and popularity—or *comfort*—eventually caused him to become careless. *Comfort can often create spiritual crisis.* This was evident when King Nebuchadnezzar constructed the elaborate city of Babylon. He had conquered Israel, destroying Jerusalem and taking the golden temple treasures for himself, and he was bragging upon his prowess and his accomplishments. Suddenly God struck him with a complete mental breakdown, and this famous king was driven into the wilderness to live like a wild animal for seven years. (See Daniel 4.)

Even Noah, after spending more than a hundred years to prepare the ark and riding out a universal flood with his family and a boat full of animals, exited the ark, planted a vineyard, and became drunk. His hard work led to a successful assignment, and when the assignment concluded, it was no longer necessary to plan for his family's survival. Thus Noah was *drunk on success*, living carelessly after the conflict. There are two times the battle will emerge: after you have experienced a great victory, and after you have experienced a stunning defeat. *The enemy comes to steal your spoil of war from your victory or to steal your faith to overcome your vice.*

## THE ROOT OF ISOLATION

I believe a third root was not just David's failed marriage, but there is also the significance of isolation—*too much time alone in the palace.* I'm certain David was weary after years of battling lions, bears, Philistines, and King Saul, and he was ready to "chill out" and let someone else deal with adversity. His separation from battle forced him into a position of isolation. The danger of isolation is that it breeds loneliness, and this loneliness gives more time for the mind to wander and for your thoughts to roam aimlessly for hours or days, eventually creating seasons of oppression, depression, or tempting thoughts.

All men were created in God's image (Gen. 1:26), and His image is expressed to human beings through the love we have toward one another. We were created to experience the emotion of fulfillment through the relationships we make with those around us and with people who love us in return. When God created Adam in the Garden of Eden, He created and surrounded him with thousands of animals. It was God who said, "It is not good that man should be alone" (Gen. 2:18). Actually Adam wasn't *alone*, as his normal day consisted of dogs barking, cats meowing, cows mooing, and roosters crowing! He lived in the world's first garden *zoo*! But the animals couldn't *kiss* him, *hug* him around the neck, and tell him "I love you." Thus, to prevent loneliness, God created a physical companion, Eve, as it was not (and is not) good for a man to be alone.

When Jacob was *alone*, he wrestled a man until the breaking of day (Gen. 32:24). Jacob's wrestling began at night and didn't conclude until the sun was rising. Using this as a spiritual example of loneliness, one reason it is not good to be alone—in isolation—is because a lonely person will wrestle with a bombardment of arrows striking the mind with no one present to talk to, share with, or help carry the weight. As the sun sets and the dark hours of the night eventually give way to the breaking of day, a person alone without love will be exhausted from all the mind wrestling. It may seem frivolous to point this out, but this is one excellent reason for a person to have a pet, some living creature in his or her home or apartment that he or she can share time and attention with. Pets, including cats, dogs, and even horses, are being used for recovery therapy.

If pets are good therapy, then I am in extremely fine emotional, mental, and physical condition! We have two cats, two pocket parrots, and a large African gray parrot whose vocabulary includes imitating the cat's meow, sounding like the ring on a cell phone, and inspiring my wife daily with the words, "Roll Tide…Roll Tide…" It is, however, rather odd when a couple, especially the female, visits the house and suddenly hears whistling…you know the kind you used to do when your wife walked into the room! Their eyes get big as if to say, "Who just whistled at me?" I look back and say, "It wasn't me!" And then I point to the living room! Pets can fill voids for lonely personalities. There are times to be alone and times we must not be alone, especially when we are in a mental struggle. One of the sins of the ancient city of Sodom was the "abundance of idleness," meaning an unsettled restlessness with nothing to do (Ezek. 16:49). Perhaps this idleness gave opportunity for the young men to spend time with the older men in the city whose lives had become filled with iniquity and who led the younger men to follow after the old men's footsteps (Gen. 19:4–5).

## YOUR OWN PRIVATE WARS

There are two types of battles: the one *easy* to win, and the one *hard* to win. The focus of the simpler battles is *distraction,* which temporarily pulls you from your intended assignment. Life is full of natural distractions, such as lightning knocking out electricity for the entire day, bringing your technical needs to a sudden deafening halt. Distraction is the hail damage that makes your young car look like it has a case of auto acne. Distractions are when storms push trees from their roots to rest peacefully on your roof. Distractions seldom defeat you—they do, however, delay you.

Numerous distractions mentally *drain* a person, just like the continual words of Delilah to Samson: "Tell me…tell me…if you love me, tell me…" (See Judges 16:6, 10, 13.) She pressed him with words until he was vexed to the point of death (v. 16). Unknowingly

*Samson was engaged in a private war that would lead to his public humiliation.*

The danger of a private war is that unless your struggle is brought to light, no one will know you are fighting it. And while you smile, showing off your pearly whites, depression is weighing you down from the inside. Your nervous laughter serves to put a curtain up over those fiery darts while you are burning with the thought to take your own life. The comment of what a great family you have might cause you to cringe inside with the thought, "I hope they never find out how dysfunctional we really are." The business success the man has in public is the talk of the town, but no one knows the alcoholic demon he hides in his desk drawer at his home office. Just as the sin of David reveals a five-part progression, there are also steps downward into the basement of private bondage.

## THE POWER OF IMAGINATION

Any private sin begins with *impressions*, thoughts that become a visible mental picture. This is the realm of *imagination* and mental images. If the imprints on your mind become a fantasy story in your head, then they will become an obsession you will pursue. Obsessions eventually forge mental strongholds, and strongholds are like walls that keep your thoughts locked in a cage in bars of your own mental prison. When mental thoughts persist over time, and these thoughts are negative, perverse, or fleshly, then the Holy Spirit will initiate a good dose of *conviction* to reprove you and move you toward repentance, cleansing, and renewing. If there is not a move toward seeking spiritual freedom and deliverance, then the adversary often releases the weapon of oppression. The enemy throws the dart to tempt you to sin; then if you do, he throws another dart (a double whammy) telling you how awful you are and how God now hates you! Mental depression can become so intense that it feels like a deep pit of despair without a ladder. Depression certainly feeds off of isolation.

One of the classical biblical examples of a descent into despair is King Saul, Israel's first king. Saul was selected by the Lord and anointed with oil by Samuel. He began on the right track and was humble before both God and men at the outset of his rule. Over time he became lifted up in pride and refused to obey the Lord. As a result, God initiated a future replacement for Saul, a young shepherd named David. We read:

> Then Samuel took the horn of oil and anointed him in the midst of his brothers; and the Spirit of the LORD came upon David from that day forward. So Samuel arose and went to Ramah. But the Spirit of the LORD departed from Saul, and a distressing spirit from the LORD troubled him.
>
> —1 SAMUEL 16:13–14

Saul's jealousy of David opened a door for a powerful evil spirit to torment his mind. Saul was recognized publicly as king, yet he was in an internal battle with private demons that would come and go at will, tormenting the king's thoughts. Saul experienced brief seasons of relief when David ministered with his harp. However, his jealousy led to his eventual demise, as he was wounded in battle and fell upon his own sword. We read:

> And when his armorbearer saw that Saul was dead, he also fell on his sword, and died with him.
>
> —1 SAMUEL 31:5

## FALLING UPON YOUR OWN SWORD

If there is one ultimate strategy of the enemy as it relates to all ministers in any fivefold ministry office (Eph. 4:11), it is to see the spiritual leader *fall upon his own sword*. The phrase "to fall upon your own sword" means that although you tell others what to do and how to live, you do not perform these duties in your own life. This is illustrated when ministers who have warned others of traps fall into these same traps themselves, or who, after preaching the dos and the don'ts of a Christian walk to others, *do the don't* they preached to others not to do.

Many years I ago I can recall a noted television minister with a well-known global ministry. In some countries in South America American visitors observed that when this minister's program was broadcast, restaurants and sports bars would switch channels from sports games to this minister's preaching. In many of these broadcasts the message was a hard-hitting word against sin, and his messages were having an impact globally and winning the lost to Christ. However, in time it was discovered that he was living contrary to his own preaching, and he fell upon his own sword. Not only did the self-inflicted sword affect him and his ministry, but also many others lost all confidence in God and the Word because of the wound caused by the *false idea* that God was unable to preserve this man from falling. For the record, Paul wrote:

> And this is why I am suffering as I do. Still I am not ashamed, for I know (perceive, have knowledge of, and am acquainted with) Him Whom I have believed (adhered to and trusted in and relied on), and I am [positively] persuaded that He is able to guard and keep that which has been entrusted to me and which I have committed [to Him] until that day.
> —2 TIMOTHY 1:12, AMP

Younger ministers and those freshly called must understand the pitfalls that come at a very early stage of ministry, as Satan puts out a threat assessment on you from the beginning and does not always wait until you are older and mature with a global ministry to make his move against you! All ministers, both male and female, should enter the ministry with a calling from God or a burden to change lives. Each minister must enter a season of *preparation*, which comes through mentoring, working in a local church, working under another ministry, or attending a Bible-based college or university. This season to prepare helps you to focus on the assignment, learn all you can about it, and sit under spiritual authority. Often, however, a younger minister becomes impatient and overanxious and desires to "expose" his or her ministry before the people.

There can be three types of exposure in ministry that do more harm than good. They are:

1. Early exposure

2. Overexposure

3. Underexposure

Exposing a young minister before large congregations or on a platform ministry can cause a novice to fall into pride and ruin his or her potential. Paul wrote of ministers in the church and said, "Not a novice, lest being puffed up with pride he fall into the same condemnation as the devil" (1 Tim. 3:6). A novice is one who is inexperienced and unskilled, and who will often not admit his or her mistakes and blunders because of too much pride.

The second level is overexposure, which if not guarded can also create pride that causes a fall. "Moreover he must have a good testimony among those who are outside, lest he fall into reproach and the snare of the devil" (v. 7).

The third category is underexposure. If a person senses a call of God and continues for months or years without any door of ministry opportunity opening, he or she will become discouraged. The absence of activity and spiritual fruit can make a person question his or her calling, quench desire, and lead to dropping out of the race. Thus, any minister who is unprepared for the warfare in the ministry may actually spiritually harm himself and others by misusing the Word of God.

For active ministers and spiritual leaders, there must be a way to expose the pitfalls before one falls into them.

There are some interesting clues in one of Christ's parables that can be practically applied to receiving freedom from the secret bondages.

> Nor do they light a lamp and put it under a basket, but on a lampstand, and it gives light to all who are in the house. Let your light so shine before men, that they may see your good works and glorify your Father in heaven.
> —MATTHEW 5:15–16

Take a completely dark room and light a single candle; the dark room will experience an orange glow of light. If a lit candle is placed under a basket, not only is the light diminished, but also it can eventually be extinguished if there is not enough air under the basket for the fire to absorb the oxygen in the atmosphere around it.

There is a danger of *hiding in the dark* or getting comfortable living in a bushel of isolation and darkness. Any counselor will tell you that the very first act a person with any addiction must do is be willing to admit "I have this problem" and openly confess and seek out someone who can get him or her out of the dark, willing to admit that the problem is serious and must be confronted. People often live in their own little "baskets," alone and isolated from other people, away from anyone who cares for them or could help them. Once the light goes out, all that remains is darkness. The basket represents the masks we hide behind—the false smiles, the fake laughs, and the phony self-deception that whispers, "You can make it by yourself."

When the light diminishes, the darkness appears. Relight the light again. Return to the simple knowledge of the Word of God.

The understanding of Scripture brings illumination and revelation that will dispel the lies and deception of the voice of the adversary. It is better to be *proactive*, acting before the battle begins, than to be *reactive*, responding when the arrows are flying. The light of truth in your soul cannot and must not be hid. The manner by which you reveal the light is for your private illumination to become your public light, and your public light to never be hidden from a world of darkness.

One minister who fell into sin made a sad but, in many instances, true statement. He said, "With my global notoriety, who could I have gone to talk to about my situation? Most men would have told others the moment I left the room, as it is difficult for some ministers to hold something in absolute confidence." I would suggest that this generation is more open than any other for people to discuss their challenges, weaknesses, and to tell how they are being attacked by the enemy. Often those in the pews are facing the same attacks as those in the pulpits. It is always good to have special friends whom you totally trust, and especially your own companion, to whom you can go to openly share your private battles with.

Many years ago when I encountered a terrible spiritual battle that was certainly demonically inspired, I tried for several months to fight it on my own, keeping the mental side of the conflict hidden under my little mental basket, only to discover no fresh light can reach the darkness when you are hiding that battle in yourself. After standing up and confessing the mental conflict to 750 people, the Lord renewed my mind and spirit and released a fresh anointing, sparing me, I am certain, from a more terrible pit in the future. Months later my precious wife asked me, "I knew something was wrong; why didn't you come to me and tell me you were depressed?" I had no answer, other than I thought I could defeat it myself, without anyone's help.

This taught me three things.

1. Remaining isolated can cause you to lose the battle. In times of war you need other soldiers with you.

2. When you expose a secret struggle to the light, the adversary has nowhere to hide and is exposed, thus weakening the oppressive thing you are battling.

3. Make yourself accountable to friends and to your companion, if you are married, for prayer covering and strength conditioning. Those who love you will stand with you before others will.

There is a way to win private battles between you and the adversary. Jesus did it in the wilderness of temptation for forty days, and you can do it through His strategy—the power of the Spirit and the Word of God.

# Chapter 4

## BREAKING THE SPIRITS OF CUTTING AND SUICIDE

HERE ARE MANY PARENTS WHO ARE UNAWARE THAT TWO of the most serious and dangerous attacks on this generation of youth are *cutting* and *suicide*. I have personally seen youth with scars on their arms where they have taken a sharp object and make a cut into their arms, just enough to bleed. The reasons vary, and I will not go into detail, other than to say that one young person said that many young people feel so dull and numb to the negative events of their lives that they do this to *feel pain and to know they are still living and have feelings*. One of the saddest moments in any ministry or family is to hear of a young person who took his or her own life because of feeling rejected in a relationship, or because he or she was being bullied and had become isolated from others.

Oddly, in the Bible there was one man who was both a *cutter* and *suicidal*. This unnamed fellow was living in the land of the Gaderenes, a region on the Syrian side of the Sea of Galilee. He was possessed with more than two thousand unclean spirits that were driving him to harm himself. Observe the wording of the verse in this narrative:

> And always, night and day, he was in the mountains and in the tombs, crying out and cutting himself with stones.
>
> —MARK 5:5

This mentally tormented man was not living with his family, with friends, or even in the community, but he was staying in the local graveyard, which metaphorically can represent *memories of past things* as graves hold no life, only memories of a past life. Notice he was awake day and night, meaning he was unable to sleep properly because of the spirits that were tormenting him day and night. The Bible also says he was "crying," but the original Greek word used in this passage is not the normal word for shedding tears when a person is sad or upset. It is the word *krazo*, which means, "to scream; to shriek and call aloud."[1] His cry was one of inner torment, screaming night and day because he was unable to free himself from his mentally tortured condition.

The phrase "cutting himself with stones" is interesting for several reasons. We read where men attempted to bind him with fetters and chains, but these devices were like toothpicks and wax as he flexed his muscles and broke the metal chains and wooden fetters from off himself. The townspeople were in great fear for their safety, seeing his violent nature.

Many times I have been to the ancient ruins in Israel where this event happened. I have seen that the stones in the area in and around Galilee are made predominantly from limestone or, in certain areas, of black volcanic rock as the region was once volcanically active. It would be difficult to do yourself permanent harm with a deep, dangerous gash by attempting to cut yourself on these stones. However, his arms and body no doubt were covered with scars and scabs, perhaps from falling over the stones in the areas or rubbing his arms violently against them like wood against sandpaper.

The point is that these spirits had seized complete mental control over this man and were motivating him to take his own life. If he had had access to a sword or knife, he would have used the weapon on himself or perhaps others.

To prove this can be called a *suicide spirit* (a spirit sending thoughts of self-destruction and hopelessness into the mind of this man), when the demons were expelled from the man, they entered into a large herd of swine, causing the wild pigs to run "violently" down a steep place, tumbling like broken rocks from an avalanche into the sea, where the entire herd choked and drowned in the water (v. 13).

There are different types of evil and unclean spirits, each with a different assignment, targeting humanity with temptations and bondages. In one biblical narrative a young boy was possessed with a spirit that caused seizures. The father confessed that the spirit would overtake his son; he had often "thrown him both into the fire and into the water to destroy him" (Mark 9:22). Here the Greek word for "destroy" does not mean just to do harm; it is the Greek word *appollumi*, which means to *fully destroy*. In the King James Version it is translated as to "die" or to "perish." In the cases of the tormented man and the young boy, these spirits were actually attempting to take the lives of their victims prematurely.

Think of the numerous times Satan made attempts to kill Jesus before His destiny could be fulfilled. After Jesus was born, King Herod send Roman soldiers to kill all infants under two years of age living in Bethlehem and the surrounding region (Matt. 2:16). Years later Satan tempted Jesus and suggested that God would protect Him if He threw Himself off the pinnacle of the temple—the high outer wall of Jerusalem on the southeastern corner.

Attempting to motivate Christ to jump was nothing less than

hoping He would commit suicide, as this jump would have splattered the body of Christ on the rocks 750 feet below. Months later, however, Christ would defy the law of gravity and walk on water, high stepping over the waves of the Sea of Galilee (Matt. 14:25). Christ was unwilling to *prove* who He was to satisfy Satan (who already knew), but He was willing to confirm who He was to His disciples!

Right after this temptation, Christ returned to Nazareth and preached His first public message, so enraging His hometown that the men rose up to throw Him off a cliff. Christ didn't willfully jump from a high place in Jerusalem, so the adversary now forced Him into a corner with no way out.

However, Christ escaped the mob and left town, headed to the lower Galilee (Luke 4:29–30). While in Galilee He was in a boat with His disciples, crossing the lake, when a sudden storm struck the boat, causing fear that they were all going to drown in the churning water. This was another occasion that put the entire ministry team in danger of a premature death at sea (Mark 4:38). Later, while Christ was ministering at the temple in Jerusalem, the people took up stones to stone Him. Once again He escaped without a scratch (John 10:31, 39).

When Satan placed the thought in the heart of Judas to betray Christ for thirty pieces of silver, I wonder if Judas, who had seen Christ escape from the enemy's hands many times, assumed Christ could or would do it again. Or did he think that if Christ was the real King of Israel, this would be His golden opportunity to rise to the occasion, overthrow the Romans, and capture the throne promised to the Messiah, the son of David? After realizing he had participated in a death plot involving shedding innocent blood, Judas threw the money back at the priests in the temple, repented to himself (meaning he had remorse), and hung himself from a tree on the edge of the Valley of Hinnom, outside of the walls of Jerusalem (Acts 1:16–19).

## THE BAAL CUTTERS

Young people often turn to cutting because they think no one is listening to them and the only way they can get attention is to do something so dramatic it will cause their parents or friends to pay attention to their pain. The false prophets of Baal had the same goal of gaining attention when they met the prophet Elijah on Mount Carmel and were challenged by him to a contest—the God who would answer by fire would be identified as the true God. As the prophets of Baal built their altar, slew their sacrifice, and began to pierce the air for several hours with cries to their god, the heavens were brass. The Bible says:

> And so it was, at noon, that Elijah mocked them and said, "Cry aloud, for he is a god; either he is meditating, or he is busy, or he is on a journey, or perhaps he is sleeping and must be awakened." So they cried aloud, and cut themselves, as was their custom, with knives and lances, until the blood gushed out on them. And when midday was past, they prophesied until the time of the offering of the evening sacrifice. But there was no voice; no one answered, no one paid attention.
> —1 KINGS 18:27–29

Just as with the cutters of Baal, oddly, several religions use cutting as a way of allegedly gaining the attention of their god. For example, here is a report given by scholars of the rites of the Hindu goddess Matha:

> There was a multitude of ten or twelve thousand people assembled. In a short time a man advanced into the center of the group, pretending that the goddess had entered into him; pulling off his turban and tossing his long hair over his

face, he began to leap and shake, uttering a noise occasionally like the bark of a dog. As his excitement increased, he beat himself with a chain, and made incisions in his tongue with a sword. Having taken the blood, he rubbed it on the foreheads of the spectators. By and by the infection spread, and others pretended to be in like manner possessed by the goddess; so that in a short time every party had three or four of the possessed. These poor, infatuated men continued to leap and shake the whole night.[2]

There are other religions in which cutting the flesh is a part of a ritual to commemorate an event or to gain attention of the particular god of their religion. Each year tens of thousands of a particular branch among the Shiite Muslims in Iraq recall the death of the seventh-century martyr Imam Hussein with a march that takes place in the city of Karbala, Iraq. There the multitude of Shiites flagellate themselves on their foreheads with swords or beat their backs with chains until blood drips down their faces and is splattered on their white shrouds. Shiites believe Hussein to be the true heir of Islam's founder, Muhammad. However, his rise to fame led to a battle in AD 680 in Karbala, where he and seventy followers were slain by the opposing Sunni Muslims.

The prophets of Baal were cutting themselves because their god (which did not exist except in their minds) was ignoring their cries for intervention. Among some of the ancient tribes the idea was that blood attracted the power of the gods, releasing supernatural energy and authority upon the worshipper. As the Baal "dance team" began preforming, they drew blood from their flesh but no attention from their god.

Physical cutting is self-abuse and self-injury. Each year one in five females and one in seven males engage in some form of self-injury.[3] A high percent of those engaged in self-injury activities have themselves experienced some form of sexual abuse. Each year in America there are two million cases of self-injury reported.[4] The root causes of self-abuse are eating disorders, depression, all forms of anxiety, drug and alcohol (substance) abuse, and relationship disorders. Among teens the most common cause of self-abuse is a broken relationship—either parents divorcing or a separation of a boy or girlfriend.

## DESTROYING THE IMAGE OF GOD

Have you ever pondered what all the numerous personal battles are really about, especially all forms of substance abuse leading to addictions? It is not just the lone stranger in the back alley whose life is being strangled to death by an addiction demon; the kids who were raised in children's church and warmed pews on Sunday mornings are also targets of these spirits of bondage. I believe a root motivation for the kingdom of darkness to attack the weakest and the strongest among us is his desire to smear and distort the image of God in us.

Our economic status, clothing quality, home size, or car costs do not impress Satan. What he sees in each person is more than the physical, outward human being. Consider a physical man. Years ago I preached a message relating that each human has a specific amount of minerals in his or her body. There is enough iron to make a nail, enough sulfur to kill all fleas on an average dog, enough carbon to make nine hundred pencils, and enough fat to make seven bars of soap.[5] If we were to add up all of the minerals in the human body (not the cells, blood, sperm—just the minerals) and sell them, we could receive about $14 for the total (estimates vary). Take the average $14 man. He wears a $200 suit, a $30 tie, and an $80 pair of shoes, and he drives a $35,000 car and lives in an $185,000 house. He goes home after work to enjoy his $14 wife and $7.50 kids (children are half the size of their parents and thus contain less mineral content)! After dinner this $14 man reclines in a $300 recliner and reads a $0.50 newspaper. He will retire at night in an $800 bed, sleep seven hours, wake up, and then repeat the same process—eating breakfast, driving to work, working, then coming home.

A preset day will come as the clock of time ticks down to his final second on earth. This man, as all other men, will go the way of the grave (Heb. 9:27). This $14 man will be clothed in a $200 suit, laid in a $1,500 coffin, and taken to graveyard where a group of men he may have never met will take a $25 shovel and cover up his physical remains with the same substance he was created from—dirt! However, it was not the dust man that Satan and his cohorts were after. Notice Ecclesiastes 8:8 and 12:7 (KJV):

> There is no man that hath power over the spirit to retain the spirit; neither hath he power in the day of death.... Then shall the dust return to the earth as it was: and the spirit shall return unto God who gave it.

Man is the only creature of any flesh form living on earth or in the cosmic realm that was purposely formed in the image and in the likeness of God.

> So God created man in his own image, in the image of God created he him; male and female created he them.
> —GENESIS 1:27, KJV

Being created in God's image means that you are a reflection of Him. Angels are spirits only, but each human born on Planet Earth is a spirit with a soul living in a body (1 Thess. 5:23). A unique and sacred gift was imparted to man that separates him from the animal kingdom. A man and woman can procreate a human who has an eternal soul and spirit, an act that no angelic being in either the kingdom of light or darkness can do.

You are also distinguished from the angels by a life-giving force that is pumped throughout your physical body, a substance called blood. Neither Satan, fallen angels, nor any angel in the heavenly realm have any form of blood within their being. While your outward man of the flesh will age and eventually perish, your inner soul and spirit are eternal, meaning they can never perish or die and thus will live on—either with God in His presence or in the lake of fire with the fallen angels and Satan (Rev. 20:14–15; 21:8).

Herein is the primary reason for Satan working against God and working to deceive and capture men and women. If you choose to enter into a redemptive covenant with Christ and you continue in your faith, you will enter the heavenly kingdom of God and gain the gift of eternal life. This is why the death of one of His children is precious in the sight of the Lord (Ps. 116:15).

Now consider the consequences of a human who passes after living in evil, wickedness, and iniquity without a saving, redemptive covenant. At the death of the unrighteous, the soul and spirit depart the body and are forever separated from God in the lower chambers under the earth.

Because the soul and spirit came from God and originated in God, who gave each human the life force to live on earth, then once the sinner is separated from God forever, *it is a part of God Himself that He never gets back, a part of Himself that is forever separated from Him!* The body of a person was formed in the womb through the miracle of cells, blood, and flesh. However, the soul and spirit are the eternal nature imparted directly from God Himself and placed within the seed and egg at the moment of conception (Jer. 1:5). Satan will use the body (addiction) to get into the mind and eventually capture the spirit.

When individuals, especially if they are of a child-bearing age, take their own life, they stop not only their future but also the lives of all of the descendants who would come out of their loins (if they are male) or out of their womb (if they are female). The example of this is when Cain killed Abel and buried him in the ground. God asked Cain where his brother was, and Cain replied, "Am I my brother's keeper?"

God replied that the "voice of your brother's blood cries out to Me from the ground" (Gen. 4:9–10).

In Hebrew the word for "blood" is plural, meaning "bloods." Why would God call one man's blood poured out as *bloods* (plural) and not *blood* (singular)? A Jewish guide in Israel explained to me that the rabbinical belief was that when Cain killed Abel, he slew not one man but an entire nation that would never be born! Thus there were voices crying out through the blood, shrieking upward to the Creator of mankind; the voices were the tens of thousands that would never be allowed to visit earth or live on the planet, because one righteous man had died. The suicide of one person causes generational homicide of entire future generations. Each living person is connected to the past (their ancestors) and the future (their unborn seed).

Can one person actually be all that important in God's eye, just one solitary life? Consider Abraham, who had no child through Sarah until he was one hundred, then Isaac was born. Isaac married at about age forty and was blessed with two sons, Esau and Jacob (Gen. 25:25–26). The patriarch Jacob saw twelve sons come through his loins who became the twelve tribal fathers of Israel. After many years seventy souls came out of Jacob (Exod. 1:5). After hundreds of years those seventy men became six hundred thousand men of war at the time of Israel's exodus from Egypt (Exod. 12:37).

Today there are more than 15 million Jews in the world, and according to some estimates there should be 200 million. However, the 6 million Jewish deaths during the Holocaust, which included 1.5 million children, caused a reduction in the Jewish population from a possible 200 million today to about 15 million who consider themselves natural-born Jews with a Jewish mother.

With all of the biblical and covenant promises that were

promised to the Jews, if Satan could wipe out the Jewish race or Israel, he could announce God a liar, as God swore by Himself to Abraham that a great nation would come from him. Thus from one man's seed emerged God's nation of promise, Israel. One seed that is conceived can reproduce in a thousand years a multitude of people.

## WHY FOLLOW A FAILURE

Most people desire to connect with a person, business, or church that is "successful" in what they are doing. I cannot understand why some men and women willfully choose to follow Satan, when his past record is one of complete failure. He was created as one of the most magnificent angelic beings, an anointed cherub, who lost his leadership position in heaven, was expelled, and is presently an unemployed cherub.

He was also assigned as a worship leader to direct the angelic host in worshipping God upon the sacred, holy mountain, yet he was booted off the mountain and excommunicated from the angelic heavenly choir. A third of the angelic hosts were deceived into following him in his rebellion, believing he could succeed in overpowering and overthrowing God and capturing God's throne room in a hostile takeover, but they were met with fierce opposition and forcibly expelled from the temple of heaven (Isa. 14:12–15; Ezek. 28:11–15; Luke 10:18). That was just his past before Adam was created! And people want to follow this failure?

Consider that, if you follow this prince of darkness, *his future is your future.* According to Scripture he will be expelled from the second heaven in a battle with the archangel Michael in the middle of the future Great Tribulation (Rev. 12). He will then have a limited time to accomplish what he wishes, but after forty-two months he will be face-to-face with one of God's messengers, who will have a chain and a key to the abyss to bind him for a thousand years (Rev. 20:1–4). After he is loosed for a season, his final doom will be in the lake of fire, where he will be confined for ages upon ages to come (vv. 10, 14). He was, is, and will continue to be an eternal loser whose obituary was recorded more than nineteen hundred years ago by John!

After Satan was expelled from heaven, God came to earth and created the first man, Adam. This new creation would become the new worshipper and would fellowship with God at the tree of life (Gen. 3:8). Satan hates you and all of mankind, especially those whose trust is in the Lord, because he views you as his replacement! When he sees you, he also can *see the image of God* that you reflect.

## The Demonic Design for Addictions

Years ago I experienced a revelation from God that Satan's purpose for leading multitudes into addiction, drunkenness, and rebellion was to *alter the image of God*! Substance abuse changes the person you actually are. When a person is high or drunk, he or she is not the "real" person, as another personality begins to emerge. Men become drunk and become child abusers and wife beaters; when mothers become addicts, they neglect their children, which is something contrary to the inbred nature of a mother.

Over the years I have spoken with literally hundreds of men and women who battled addictions and now are free through the power of God. When asking them why they turned to drugs and alcohol, about nine out of ten gave me the same answer. They replied, "I did it to dull the pain and the hurts I was feeling in my life."

After hearing this response over and over for many years, I then saw another aspect of Satan's strategy. By keeping a person high or drunk, the enemy is also dulling them to the point where they *cannot feel* the joy and peace that come from the presence of God. The presence of God is not emotions, but there is an emotional response when a person feels the power of God, especially for the first time. The deader you are on the inside, the less likely you are to sense the force of spiritual conviction of sin from the Holy Spirit and even less likely to be able to feel the peace and joy that emit from the Holy Spirit's presence. You will eventually become lulled to sleep and dulled to death. Substance abuse is a false "high" leading to a deadly low.

Thousands of individuals of all ages have been released from suicidal thoughts and self-abuse after hearing a "testimony" of how Christ delivered others from similar bondages. A believer has a great power resource that can construct a shield of faith in a person whose trust was burned by fiery arrows of bondages when someone now freed from the same prison house of death shares their personal testimony. A testimony gives evidence that God is willing and able to deliver those who ask and believe. Paul stood before Roman leaders and gave the testimony of his life before and after Christ, often bringing listeners to conviction and at times stirring up religious Pharisees to the point of desiring Paul dead. The religious Jews who rejected Christ as Messiah were threatened by Paul's conversion as the apostle was a leading and well-respected Jewish rabbi prior to his Damascus Road conversion.

You can overcome Satan by "the blood of the Lamb and by the word of [your] testimony" (Rev. 12:11). Your testimony is a weapon of war, a flaming arrow that can penetrate and melt the hardest heart. It is your *testimony* that can become the seed of influence and influence and lead others to follow your example. If the adversary can mar your testimony, he can sever your influence among those who are watching you to see if you truly live the life you are preaching that they should live. A strong testimony can be the first key to open the door of release for those in spiritual captivity.

Cutters and many who have suicidal thoughts are in instant need of three things from a caring, loving person or group of individuals. The first thing is love and concern. Never take lightly a child or youth saying they are being bullied at school, a girl in her room crying because of a broken relationship, or a man depressed because he lost his job. At this moment they do not need to be isolated; they need a friend to talk to them and keep their mind active with other things, not sitting alone in sorrow and pain.

Second, the friend or group must see if they can intervene in the situation that has created the negative thoughts. Great encouragement is needed, and a reminder that things will not always be as they are and God has a good plan for their life.

Third, above all they need to be ministered to spiritually so they can receive a renewing of joy, peace, and a new sense of faith. This comes through the Holy Spirit and the Word of God.

Jesus suddenly showed up in a man's life who was being driven to suicidal tendencies and cutting by evil spirits. When the spirits were cast out, the man was "sitting and clothed and in his right mind" (Mark 5:15). When you receive the redemptive covenant and allow Jesus into your situation, the tangible presence of Christ fills your heart and atmosphere, bringing rest (sitting), covering you with His presence (clothing you), and renewing you with a sound mind.

At our OCI Gathering Place in Cleveland, Tennessee, we have a Tuesday night service geared toward bringing people closer to God and seeing the oppressed go free through anointed music, preaching, and altar ministry. As I wrote earlier in this chapter, I have discovered two things about cutters and those who feel on the verge of suicide. Both have usually experienced broken relationships and feelings of hopelessness. It is the responsibility of individual believers to reach out in unconditional love to those whose emotions are crushed and hearts are broken, letting the love of God be the balm that brings healing.

When Christ preached His first sermon in Nazareth, He quoted from Isaiah 61, when He said:

The Spirit of the Lord is upon me, because he hath anointed me to preach the gospel to the poor; he hath sent me to heal the brokenhearted, to preach deliverance to the captives, and recovering of sight to the blind, to set at liberty them that are bruised.

—LUKE 4:18, KJV

Christ came to bring deliverance to the "captives." The Greek word used in this passage means, "someone taken as a prisoner of war by the point of a spear." These prisoners in Satan's kingdom are captive to their own carnal desires, which are birthing seeds of destruction. Christ also heals the brokenhearted. The Greek word for "brokenhearted" is *suntribo*; it means, "to utterly crush, to shatter, and break in pieces." The analogy is of a beautiful clay vessel that is dropped on the floor and has shattered into many pieces.

Broken relationships and betrayals lead to inner feelings of sorrow, grief, and pain. Christ sets at liberty those who are *bruised*, those who are crushed. The Spirit of the Lord releases a special anointing to minister to the *captives, brokenhearted,* and *bruised*.

This fact should be a source of encouragement to those who feel rejected, betrayed, and alone. The same Christ who delivered the man of Gadera from his demonic strongholds will deliver anyone who will fall down and begin to worship Him!

*Chapter 5*

# HUMAN CRACKS in
# VESSELS of HONOR

⋉⋊⋉⋊

MANY YEARS AGO MY EVANGELISTIC MEETINGS WOULD extend from one week to an average of three weeks in every church. At times they were like a marathon and would continue for five to eleven weeks—sometimes every night! In the late 1990s our ministry was growing, so we hired staff to assist us in filling orders, answering the mail, and designing graphics for our Voice of Evangelism (VOE) magazines, along with other important ministry related activities. Being so long out of the office made it quite difficult on both myself and our staff, as when I returned home I often had one day on the schedule to get caught up from weeks of mail and to prepare for the next revival. It also created an excellent opportunity for stress levels to rise.

On one occasion I had preached for three weeks and had one day to work in the office, so I required the staff to stay extra hours to get the work done. One of our employees was to help me answer my personal mail. I discovered she had spent about twenty-five minutes on a personal call with some friends. I was tired, irate, and frustrated, as valuable time was slipping away. I went into the office and, as the old expression says, "laid into her" for wasting time and not focusing on her job. She ran into the bathroom crying. I called my wife and told her about the incident. My wife said, "If she's that upset, then you have probably lost a worker." Not only did she step down a few weeks later, but she also drew others into her offense, saying negative things about us to her family and closest friends. In retrospect, there was a crack in my armor, and I was exposed to anger as the crack grew larger. I did apologize for my outburst; however, in life some rifts become canyons, becoming difficult to cross.

At times Christians become disappointed in their pastors and ministers when they begin to see the *human cracks in the chosen vessels*. To avoid being hurt, most pastors and ministers have very few close friends within their own churches, as they have learned people are apt to turn against them after consistently observing their *humanity* more than their *spirituality*. Christ had twelve disciples. However, there were occasions when He had only three—Peter, James, and John—to join Him at more spiritually intimate moments, while the other nine remained behind. This is interesting for the following reasons.

On the Mount of Transfiguration the *glory* of God covered Christ as He personally met with Israel's two greatest prophets: Elijah and Moses. Instead of all twelve disciples being present, the inner circle three—Peter, James, and John—were present and honored to view Christ at the peak of His power, His ministry, and His glory. These three could have the "bragging rights" of being allowed in a place where others were not. This would compare today to close ministry partners who have been with the pastor or evangelist from the earliest days when the crowds were low, the offerings scarce, and nothing but prayer and faith to undergird the ministry. After years of growth they are now invited to sit on the front row in special VIP seating in a new facility where thousands are attending and to talk about how they have been with you when there was nothing but a Bible and faith in God.

Switch the scene from the *Mount* of Transfiguration to a small eastern *valley* called the Garden of Gethsemane, located at the edge of the Kidron Valley in Jerusalem. Christ instructed eight of His personal disciples to remain near the edge of the garden, but He invited Peter, James, and John to go *a little farther*, deeper into the garden (Matt. 26:36–39). These three *inner-circle* disciples were allowed to witness Christ as He endured the agony of His coming death, as His sweat became like great drops of blood (Luke 22:44). Where were Moses and Elijah now? Where is that white glory cloud that engulfed Christ and the voice from heaven bragging on him, calling Him "Son" (Matt. 17:1–6)? Christ has gone from the days of grace and *glory* on a mountain to the hour of testing in the valley of *gore* and sweat mixed with blood. Soon, all but one disciple, John, would forsake Him.

Large crowds will follow your ministry when you are providing fish sandwiches and miracles are flowing! At the crucifixion, where were the same five thousand men whom Christ fed (Matt. 14:19–21), or the seventy men He called to go forth and heal the sick and cast out devils (Luke 10:1)? It's easier to *receive* a blessing than to *impart* a blessing. What happened to the multitudes who were crying *Hosanna* and waving palms, when Jesus is now in the crisis point of His life, about to hang between heaven and earth, forsaken by all men except His favorite disciple and His mother, both who stood at the cross (John 19:26–27)?

Christ was strong, wise, bold, and anointed. To Christ's casual followers, things were not supposed to end with His violent death! According to the wise men, wasn't He born the King of the Jews (Matt. 2:2)? Where is this King's bodyguards, this King's army, this

King's secret angelic rescue team to provide a way of escape from the death sentence Christ faced? His birth gained the attention of heaven as angels sang and a loving visitation by common shepherds who had been watching their flocks but were now coming to view the infant destined to become the Great Shepherd. As a King He was visited by wise men with expensive gifts, but as a human His birth occurred in a stable. *He could walk on water with His divinity, but His own sweat became as blood in His humanity.* The multitudes forsook Him when they discovered that His miraculous power did not deliver Him from His own enemies.

The same is true with a minister of the gospel. When his own preaching cannot deliver him from his personal "demons," then the congregation disperses, cuts off the sound system, and turns off the lights, moving on to another shepherd in another pasture. The wounded sheep are heard bleating out, "He didn't practice what he preached," or "He was a hypocrite." Instead of complaining that he didn't practice what he preached, we should ponder why what he preached didn't defeat some of what's being practiced.

The answer is not simple; there's not one answer that can explain the various failures. In and of itself the Bible is simply a book of printed words with a leather cover, *as long as it just sits on the coffee table.* When the book is read only for history, it becomes stories and instruction for the reader. However, if the words in the Bible are energized by faith and made alive to the reader by the quickening energy of the Holy Spirit, then they become effective and life transforming! The Bible can be preached and not believed, or preached and not practiced. Unless the words in the Bible are acted upon by the person who reads them, they will have no impact upon that person or upon the members and ministers in a church.

Many times a well-known and respected minister or evangelist has stood at the pinnacle of world recognition, only to be thrust into a pit of despair as the result of a moral failure or a self-inflicted sin. When that happens, his most loyal followers begin scattering from him like frightened people fleeing the radiation from a leaking power plant. These human cracks in chosen vessels are one thing to endure in *private*, but they are quite another thing when exposed in *public*.

As believers we must realize that men of God are first *men* and then *men of God*. When Christ chose His twelve disciples, many were professional fishermen, familiar with catching fish. Jesus gave instructions to follow Him, and He would make them fishers of men (Matt. 4:19). Jesus had to first *take* them before He could *make* them—forming character that would endure crisis. It took forty-two months of continual on-the-job training, and when the crisis of the crucifixion arrived, one (Judas) killed himself, one (Peter) cursed and denied Christ, and one (Thomas) didn't believe Christ was raised from the dead. Imagine three of the twelve original trainees for the ministry—one dead (Judas), one fled (Peter), and one turning red from the embarrassment of his unbelief (Thomas). Believers tend to look at a person's *present integrity* to judge his or her *future success*. What if we were to dig into a person's past and then judge that person's future success based upon pre-Christ conversion?

My grandfather related this story many years ago. A church was in need of a pastor. One of the elders was interested in knowing what kind of minister they desired. He therefore wrote a letter, writing as if he was an applicant for the position. He read this letter before the pulpit committee:

> Gentlemen,
>
> Understanding that your pulpit is vacant, I would like to apply for the position. I have many qualifications that I think you would appreciate. I have been blessed to preach with power and have had some success as a writer. Some say I am

a good organizer. I have been a lender in most places I have gone.

Some folks, however, have some things against me, as I am over fifty years old. I have never preached in one place for more than three years at a time. In some places I have left town after my work caused riots and disturbances. I have to admit that I have been in jail three or four times, but not because of any real wrongdoing. My health is not too good, but I still get a good deal done. I have had to work my trade to help pay my way. The churches I have reached have been small, though located in several large cities. I haven't gotten along too well with the other religious leaders in many towns. In fact, some of them have threatened me, taken me to court, and even attacked me physically because of my preaching. I am not too good at keeping records and have even been known to forget whom I baptized. However, if you can use me, I shall do my best for you, even if I have to work to help with my support.

The elder read this letter to the committee and asked them if they were interested in the applicant. Each replied that he would never work in their church. They were not interested in an unhealthy, middle-aged, trouble-making, absentminded ex-jailbird. In fact, they felt insulted that such a person would send an application for the pastorate to their respected, uptown church, which was known for powerful New Testament preaching. The committee finally asked the name of the applicant. "The apostle Paul," the elder answered, as the committee members sat silently, with many lowering their head in embarrassment. *Each believer should be appreciative that God does not consult the past to determine the future.*

All ministers of the gospel must balance a life between two worlds—the natural and the spiritual. In the morning they are a husband and father. At noon they are a counselor heading up the staff meeting, and by night they are a communicator of the gospel and a shepherd. They wear the bishop's robe, exchange it for the shepherd's robe, then for a pair of pajamas at home where the *preacher* is simply *Daddy* to his children. We expect the preacher to smile all the time, be patient without complaining, happy and never sad, and able to take criticism without responding. We want him to be like Jesus, and certainly that should be every minister's goal. However, Jesus's kindness was turned to anger when He overthrew the tables of the money changers (Matt. 21:12–13). His patience ran low with the Pharisees, and He chose such bold words as "hypocrites" to describe these snakes in the synagogues (Matt. 6:16). Critics were also confronted when they challenged Christ's credibility.

Believers must acknowledge that all soldiers of the faith—from the older *generals* who run global missions programs or megachurch outreaches, to the *private first class* who cares for the infants in the nursery—are vulnerable to tiredness, discouragement, illness, and satanic assaults. After many years of full-time traveling ministry to churches in thirty-five states and personally meeting ministers and members who were beat up from the battle, I found seven factors that wear down believers and can produce cracks in vessels of honor.

## BEWARE OF DISTRACTIONS

The Roman soldier was vulnerable to tiredness, illness, and many non-battle adversities that could wear him down. The Christian soldier is also vulnerable to forces and situations that can needlessly drain energy and bring mental distractions. Here are seven of the most common factors that can wear down our spiritual strength.

### I. NOT RECEIVING A FRESH ANOINTING IN A NEW BATTLE

Every new conflict needs a fresh anointing. When the methods and strategies against you change, then the level of anointing for battle must change. David's progression of battles began with a bear, then a lion, then a giant, followed by the Philistine nation. First there was the bear. A bear's danger is in its claws, but a lion's strength is its mouth. A giant such as Goliath made a threat showing his large weapons, and the Philistines could intimidate with their large numbers of soldiers. The anointing is the inner power of God that abides in a Spirit-filled believer and is released in moments of ministry or as necessary when dealing with the powers of the enemy. Just as light can go out when the ancient lamps ran out of oil, a neglected prayer life can cause the fire to die and the anointing to decline. When the battle is on, then the presence of God must be your life source and the armor your protection.

## 2. REPLACING PRAYER WITH PRAISE

A prophetic warning was given around 1906, during the Azusa Street revival, that basically said in the last days the church would come to a place where they would *worship* a God they would not pray to. The spiritual emphasis would be on *worship* and not on *prayer*. When the music is appealing, the sound system good, and the singers' harmony mesmerizing, believers can sit or at times stand endlessly to enjoy the best sound in town. But try to inspire the same group when calling for a one-hour intercession service where they can talk face-to-face with God! The crowds disperse and the prayer service is attended by the faithful few. Pay attention...we cannot survive a battle without knowing how to pray! Ephesians 6:18 tells us to pray "always with all prayer and supplication in the Spirit, being watchful to this end with all perseverance and supplication for all the saints."

In an earlier chapter I mentioned that prayer is like the javelin the Roman soldier shot at the enemy before going into battle. When you praise, it ascends to heaven and remains, but when you pray, what goes up will eventually come back down! *Praise benefits God, but prayer benefits you.*

### 3. TAKING ON UNASSIGNED BATTLES

Carnal people who have no relationship with God can be *dumpers.* They want to dump the blame on you, their problems on you, their financial obligations on you, and they dump what they don't want on whoever will carry their trash for them. That is not to say we are to avoid being compassionate and caring for someone away from God or unwilling to follow Him. However, don't put yourself under self-imposed burdens or self-invited oppression. Do not take on everybody else's problems or any unnecessary cares God did not assign to you. With faith and prayer, deal with solutions to your own problems; handle your own family's crisis and any other battles that God permits you to encounter—but never be pulled into another person's battle just for the battle's sake.

### 4. GOING WHERE WE ARE NOT CALLED

There is a difference between being *called* and being *burdened.* For example, you might have a burden for foreign evangelism or foreign missions, but that does not necessarily mean that you are called to be a missionary and permanently live in a particular nation. Your calling might be to oversee prayer teams, organize missions groups, or provide financial support for others to make a missions journey. During my ministry I have seen men and women have a God encounter that turned their world upside down. In their zeal to follow God, they began seeking what ministry they could do for the kingdom. At times their zeal exceeded their wisdom, and they quit school, quit their job, or made a sudden transition when no doors were opened. *Stay where you have been planted, grow where you stay, and create fruit while you grow.* God has the keys to lock and unlock doors, so don't force doors open that are shut or shut doors that are opened.

5. SPENDING MORE TIME WITH MEN THAN WITH GOD

After being called into the ministry, I was still a teenager traveling to small, rural churches and preaching to mostly Christians. One of my spiritual mentors, a man mightily used of God to demonstrate His power, called me into his office and said, "Perry, if you are to be used by God, you need to spend more time with God than with men." His words pierced my spirit, and I felt convicted for my lack of prayer time. From that moment forward, and to this day, my average day includes spending eight to ten hours in study and prayer or meditating upon the Lord—usually a combination of all three. If you're not careful and watchful, your social network life will replace your prayer time. When you are consumed with men, you will think like men; when you are consumed with God, you will think like God.

6. FIGHTING THE WRONG WAR

My wife has a Facebook page and is often amused and at times shocked at the reaction to different articles or comments she posts. It is very clear that a large number of Christians not only do not know what they are fighting, but also they are actually fighting in the wrong war. They believe their war is with another Christian who believes differently than they do, or their struggle is over a particular doctrinal issue on which they disagree. Others are self-appointed watchdogs of the faith and believe they are called to defend their positions, which, of course, are the only right interpretations of the Scripture. When one denomination attacks another, and one ministry another, the enemy laughs and enjoys a mini-vacation, knowing that sinners will never be attracted to a church that specializes in fighting each other.

7. USING THE WRONG WEAPONS

God has given us the weapons to tear down strongholds—the inward strongholds that take our thought life captive and the outward strongholds that form addictions and bondages in our life. The Bible says:

> For though we walk in the flesh, we do not war according to the flesh. For the weapons of our warfare are not carnal but mighty in God for pulling down strongholds, casting down arguments and every high thing that exalts itself against the knowledge of God, bringing every thought into captivity to the obedience of Christ.
>
> —2 Corinthians 10:3–5

## Four Strategies

Now that we know seven factors that can wear us down, here are four strategies that help us overcome in these end-time battles.

### 1. The Word must be spoken and not just thought upon.

Since the darts of Satan are sent against the human mind, and the battlefield is the mind, then the Word of God must not just be mused in the mind; it must be spoken. The reason is that what is within the heart and mind will manifest in the words of the mouth. There are some things that tempt one person that may not tempt another, because they are not at all in the person's heart. *Fiery darts can only set on fire what has already had fuel placed upon it.* Long before a harvest of failure occurs, the seeds of defeat were planted in the field of the mind and spirit. Since the mouth speaks what is implanted in the mind, then God's Word must be audibly spoken.

Christ is the example of speaking the written Word aloud to cut into the mental attack of Satan (Matt. 4:1–10). During Christ's temptation three different arrows were shot at Him. Each time Christ quoted the Scriptures to quench the fiery missile. If Satan planted the dart in Christ's mind, Christ canceled it out when He spoke the Word into the atmosphere. *The spoken Word of God is always superior to the spoken words of Satan.* The concealed power in each word is released when mixed with faith and spoken with authority!

2. A BELIEVER CAN USE PERSONAL PROPHECY AS A WEAPON.

When Paul wrote to Timothy, he instructed him:

> This charge I commit to you, son Timothy, according to the prophecies previously made concerning you, that by them you may wage the good warfare, having faith and a good conscience, which some having rejected, concerning the faith have suffered shipwreck.
>
> —1 TIMOTHY 1:18–19

Timothy was a young pastor ministering among older, established believers, some who considered him too young for this type of large ministry (1 Tim. 4:12). Apparently there was a confrontation with certain elders, as Timothy is instructed not to rebuke an elder (1 Tim. 5:1). Timothy was experiencing a *spirit of fear*, or in the Greek, a *spirit of timidity or intimidation*, resulting from this conflict. When Timothy was commissioned to Ephesus by Paul, the presbyters had laid hands upon Timothy and imparted spiritual gifts. Paul instructed Timothy, "Do not neglect the gift that is in you, which was given to you by prophecy with the laying on of hands of the eldership" (1 Tim 4:14). This verse indicates that the Holy Spirit used Paul to give Timothy a prophetic word, and Paul instructed his spiritual son to war, or win this battle, with the prophecies that went before him when the Spirit had indicated Timothy was called and assigned to this church.

When struggling with verbal, mental, and physical attacks, including temptations, Christ is our example as He quoted the Word of God to resist Satan's mental darts (Matt. 4:1–10). When you have a true prophetic word spoken over your destiny, when the enemy attempts to steal your future, you must recall the words and promise the Holy Spirit has given and fight with the prophecies that have gone before you. This includes spiritual dreams, visions, and personal words given to you by the Holy Spirit.

### 3. WE MUST FIGHT WITH THE KNOWLEDGE OF GOD'S WILL (HEB. 10:36).

This is a powerful concept. Being in the will of God means that nothing can get past God, surprise God, or even affect your destiny unless it is permitted in the will of God. The *will of God* is God's predesigned purpose for your life. The will of God is being what you are, who you are, where you are at the time. Since the steps of a good man are ordered of the Lord (Ps. 37:23), then each part of your life is directed, even when the circumstances seem otherwise. Job was still in God's will even when he lost his children, wealth, and health.

Years ago a noted minister had a major heart attack and was near death's door. His boss was a noted minister who prayed for the sick and saw great miracles. The minister came to the hospital ICU, bent over, and asked his colleague, "Do you believe God is finished with you?" The man slowly nodded no. The second question was, "Do you believe it is God's will to heal you?" He slowly nodded in the affirmative. The minister prayed a mighty prayer of faith, and the man was raised from his deathbed and lived on for many years. *He battled his way from death to life with the knowledge of God's will!* When you know who you are, what you are, where you are going, and how you are getting there because you know God's will, then the enemy cannot move you. You and God know the plan and purpose of your life.

### 4. GUARD THE WORDS FROM YOUR MOUTH (PROV. 18:21; MARK 7:20–23).

I will be the first to confess two things about myself that I do not like and have to continually work on. First, I tend to say too much. At times I give too much information, and at times I share my feelings—when I should simply shut up. The second is that I tend to speak up very quickly, giving an opinion first and thinking later, instead of thinking first and then speaking. *I have discovered the hard way that you will never have to remember words that you never said or recall negative words that were never spoken!* In the New Testament James said much about the tongue (or words).

James in his epistle was dealing with Christian living and conduct. In chapter 1 he emphasized the importance of enduring testing and temptation. In chapter 2 he taught how to treat one another in the church with equal respect and the need to combine faith and action to demonstrate that you are truly a believer. In chapter 3 he wrote about disciplining your tongue and controlling what you say.

James chose three different analogies in James 3 to demonstrate to the reader the importance of self-control: a *bit*, a *rudder*, and a *spark of fire* (vv. 3–6). The bit is placed in the mouth of a horse to control the direction of the entire body of the animal. The rudder is built on the back of a ship, and by the captain turning the rudder the entire ship's direction can be determined. One small spark has caused massive fires, burning hundreds of acres that cannot be controlled once the fire spreads. A bit is small compared to a horse, a rudder is small compared to the entire ship, and a spark seems like nothing when compared to the entire fire. So the tongue is a small member of the body, but it can cause more damage at times than an entire wild fire! Men can tame a wild bear and a lion yet have difficulties taming their own tongues. Proverbs 18:21 says, "Death and life are in the power of the tongue." The apostle Peter added, "He who would love life and see good days, let him refrain his tongue from evil, and his lips from speaking deceit" (1 Pet. 3:10).

An untamed tongue "sets on fire the course of nature" (James 3:6). The Greek word for "course" here is *trochos*; it means, "a wheel," referring to a circuit that a runner runs or the circuit of human life. The Greek word for "nature" means, "procreation, birth, and nativity." The phrase refers to the wheel or life process set in motion from the moment of birth, continuing throughout our entire life. From the beginning of life images are implanted in our minds because of words. Men and women are incarcerated today because when they were a child or teen, someone set their mind and spirits on fire with negative or dangerous words, which set in motion a wheel of destruction, moving them from one destructive event to another. Whoever said "Sticks and stones may break my bones, but words will never hurt me" apparently was never insulted or abused, cursed or ridiculed by words, because negative and hateful words will crush the spirit and build mental strongholds in the mind.

There are various types of words, including bitter words (Ps. 64:3), hateful words (Ps. 109:3), flattering words (Prov. 2:16), grievous words (Prov. 15:1), and wounding words (Prov. 18:8). On the other hand there are truthful words (Prov. 22:21), words of knowledge (Prov. 19:27), pleasant words (Prov. 15:26), and wise words (Prov. 23:9). The spiritual condition and attitude of a speaker will determine if either bitter or sweet water will flow from their words. We are informed, "Do not be rash with your mouth...let your words be few" (Eccles. 5:2). James later wrote that we should give an answer of simply yes or no so that we do not engage in a conversation that will eventually lead to some form of condemnation (James 5:12).

James taught that if you can bridle your tongue and not offend others with your words, then you are a "perfect man" (James 3:2). Only through divinely inspired wisdom that comes from above can a person rule over the most unruly member of our bodies—the tongue (v. 8). Wise men and women are known by their good conversations and good works (v. 13). Our prayer should always be, "Let the words of my mouth and the meditation of my heart be acceptable in Your sight, O LORD, my strength and my Redeemer" (Ps. 19:14). Someone said we should always think before we speak, but there are times when, to avoid argument and confrontation, we simply should "agree with [our] adversary quickly" (Matt. 5:25) and move on before the sparks from the tongue ignite a firestorm that cannot be quenched.

Occasionally good people will be exposed with a crack or a weakness. This, however, does not exempt them from being used of God, as God seldom uses perfect vessels, instead choosing willing and obedient vessels. Extend forgiveness and mercy to those whose battles have split their armor, dented their reputations, and wounded their souls. *You will never know when you may need the same mercy you are extending to others.* Paul reminds believers:

> Brethren, if any person is overtaken in misconduct or sin of any sort, you who are spiritual [who are responsive to and controlled by the Spirit] should set him right and restore and reinstate him, without any sense of superiority and with all gentleness, keeping an attentive eye on yourself, lest you should be tempted also.
>
> —GALATIANS 6:1, AMP

Treat all spiritual and moral soldiers who desire to recover from their wounds in the same manner that you would desire to be treated if you were in that situation. We have lost too many spiritual warriors over the years because we have allowed them to die in their own blood while attempting to heal a self-inflicted wound. The US military will go into live fire to rescue a wounded soldier and get him medical help, and the military is a brotherhood. May the church learn this lesson from our military—never leave a wounded soldier behind to die.

## Chapter 6

# WHEN BELIEVERS
# BEGIN FAINTING

I N Luke 18 Christ gave a parable of a woman who went
to an unjust judge, begging him to avenge her of her adversary.
The judge consistently ignored her, but realizing that she would
never let him rest as she did not cease to petition him, he gave
her the request of her heart. Emphasizing the persistence of the
woman, we read these words, "Men always ought to pray and not
lose heart" (Luke 18:1). The King James Version says, "Men ought
always to pray, and not to faint." The general meaning of fainting,
in a spiritual sense, means to become fainthearted, lose heart, or
feel a sense of despair.

The idea of becoming faint means, "to relax or to loosen up or to
lose altogether."[1] The ancient idea here is to loosen the string on a
bow. Once the string is loosened, you may still have a bow handle
but no strength in the bow to shoot arrows. It can also hold the
idea of being *small souled*, meaning weak in your mind. When individuals became weary and faithless, they lose their desire to fight

in a crisis, as the problems look bigger than their ability to challenge them.

Paul wrote in Galatians, "Let us not grow weary while doing good" (Gal. 6:9). Being weary in a war, a personal struggle, a failing marriage, or in dealing with rebellious children is understandable. But how can we be weary in doing good ("well doing," KJV)? Doing good should release joy and peace, not weariness. However, having completed more than three decades of ministry, I know that weariness in ministry is common. Most people know me either because I've ministered in their church or from watching the *Manna-Fest* telecast, so I'm using myself as an example. If I am at the office Monday through Thursday, there are articles to write for the Internet and magazine; books to write; e-mails to answer; studying for conferences; messages for DVDs, CDs, and meetings with staff; building projects; and hosting the weekly prayer meetings and Tuesday night services. Besides these activities, there is the weight of the finances required to maintain a ministry reaching 249 nations of the world. At times I have sat at a computer so long that when I went home and attempted to sleep, I could still see the outline of the computer when I closed my eyes! Solomon wrote, "Much study is wearisome to the flesh" (Eccles. 12:12). For a pastor, when the sheep become restless, sick, or agitated, his energy can become drained by the demands of daily ministry.

The spirit of fainting and becoming weary in well doing eventually leads to weariness, and weariness unchecked can eventually invite into your life a spirit of weakness and discouragement. In Proverbs 13:12 we read, "Hope deferred makes the heart sick." The Hebrew word for "deferred" means, "to delay, to prolong or to draw something out for a long time." As an example, when a person is taken hostage in a foreign nation, that person may spend months in a prison cell, not reading a paper, seeing the news, or hearing a report that indicates the world's news media are reporting his or her plight. Without the hope of a negotiation, the longer the captivity, the more the sense of hope is delayed, and the soul becomes sick. The common Old Testament Hebrew word for "sick" is *chalah*. The root word can mean, "to rub worn."[2] Thus the continuing pressures of life begin to wear down the mind, body, and spirit of a person to a level of total tiredness and weakness.

It reminds me of how raindrops continually dropping on a section of asphalt can eventually wear a dent or small hole in the black tar substance, or how small grains of sand blasted against granite with compressed air can actually carve letters into the hard rock. A small tree can reach for the sunlight through a crack in concrete when it's as small as a weed, but in years to come the roots underneath the cement will cause the hard concrete surface to buckle from a *root* force underground, hidden from the natural eyes. For a season we may hide our own roots of bitterness and other spiritual hindrances deep in our spirit, but eventually any planted root will produce some form of fruit—and in this case, bitterness breeds rebellion.

We know this because in Proverbs 17:11 the Hebrew word for "rebellion" is *meriy* and figuratively means, "bitterness."[3] *Marah*, which is Hebrew for "rebel," means, "to make bitter."[4] Thus a rebellious person is rooted in some form of bitterness, and a bitter person will eventually become rebellious. Every bad root will eventually produce the branches to grow bad fruit.

Once bitterness breeds rebellion, then rebellion is the door for a feeling of hopelessness, and hopelessness can lead to a desire to give up and quit. People seldom quit when they feel good about themselves or their families, love their jobs, have money in the bank, and can relax and drink hot tea at their new house on the lake. However, when crisis strikes and the marriage is in ruins, or the pink slip has been given at work and they are down to their last dollar, mental depression and a spirit of no hope can attack them.

What is the one theme that runs throughout the Bible in the lives of people who were in trouble and had to "tie a knot at the end of the rope and hold on"? It is revealed in the parable of the woman and the judge in Luke 18, which reveals that the woman persistently and consistently *cried out* to the judge.

## AVENGED OF YOUR ADVERSARY

Who is your adversity in life? The woman in Luke 18 cried out for the judge to "avenge me of mine adversary" (v. 3, KJV). The Greek word for "avenge" here means, "to vindicate, retaliate or punish."[5] The woman was asking the judge to vindicate her and punish her adversary. Later, the judge stated he will "avenge her" (v. 5). This is the same Greek word used in verse 3, meaning to vindicate and punish. However, when Christ gave His answer, He said, "And shall not God avenge his own elect, which cry day and night unto him, though he bear long with them? I tell you that he will avenge them speedily" (vv. 7–8, KJV). Here the word *avenge* is used twice; however, the Greek is a different word carrying a different meaning than the word in verse 3. The Greek word for "avenge" in verses 7 and 8 is *poieo*, and it has a wide variety of applications, including "to make or to do."[6] This woman wanted retaliation for injustice, but Christ is saying God will make justice happen, or He will *move on your behalf* when you cry out to Him! God will not *destroy* your adversary but will help you to *overcome* your adversary. Paul said it this way: "Beloved, do not avenge yourselves, but rather give place to wrath; for it is written, 'Vengeance is Mine, I will repay,' says the Lord" (Rom. 12:19–20).

The parable indicates that a person crying out can gain the attention of the judge. Just what does it mean to "cry" out to the Lord? "Crying" and "crying out" are found in various forms about 199 times in the Bible with 29 references referring to, "crying unto the Lord" (Exod. 14:10; 15:25; 17:4, and others). There are numerous examples of crying out unto the Lord; however, there are three primary examples listed below.

The first is to cry out to the Lord because of danger, grief, and anguish. When Peter began sinking under the rolling waves of the sea, he cried out to the Lord in a three-word emergency petition saying, "Lord, save me!" (Matt. 14:30). These three words were enough for Christ to *pull* him out, *pick* him up, and *walk* him back onto the ship.

The second example of crying unto the Lord is when a large multitude of people begin to cry out in unity, lifting up their voices, as in the case with Israel when they saw Pharaoh's army rumbling in their direction at the Red Sea (Exod. 14:10). Their unified crying out sent the rod in Moses's hand over the water, opening a path of escape for the entire Jewish nation.

The third example is when a person cries out for help and assistance, or as a warning. During Christ's ministry it was common for the sick to hear that Christ was near them and suddenly cry out with a loud voice to seize His attention, drawing attention to their affliction (Mark 9:24–27). In English when we say to "cry out," we picture a person yelling at the *top of their lungs* with a very loud voice.

It is interesting to see in the New Testament the different Greek words translated as "cried" and how each has a unique emphasis.

- At times when men cried out to be healed, the word is *krazo*, which means, "to croak, scream, shriek or to call out loud." This was done to get Christ's attention.[7]

- At the cross Christ *cried* out, and this word is *anaboao*, referring to, "a shout for help in a troublesome situation" (Matt. 27:46).[8]

- Another time on the cross when Christ cried out, *phoneo* is used, which is, "to cry aloud, to call, to send for, summon" (Luke 23:46).[9]

Each human has three distinct parts: a body, soul, and spirit. A cry from the body is often a result of physical pain, and the cry at a funeral or at a loss through a death reveals the agony of the human soul. In Romans Paul also identifies an odd form of communication called "groanings which cannot be uttered" (Rom. 8:26). This form of utterance is from the depth of the human spirit of a person. At times the weight and burden in the human spirit becomes so strong that when a person begins to cry out, it forms more of a groaning, a sigh, a murmur or words, or a prayer that is inaudible in human words (Rom. 8:23; 2 Cor. 5:2, 4).

It is important to understand that God responds and reaches out to those who cry out unto Him! The following chart references some of those in the Bible who cried unto the Lord and the reaction of the Lord on their behalf:

| Those Who Cried Out | Bible Reference | How God Responded |
| --- | --- | --- |
| Israel cried in bondage. | Exodus 2:23–25 | God remembered His covenant and acknowledged the people's cry. |
| Israel cried at the Red Sea. | Exodus 14:10–23 | God opened the Red Sea for them. |
| Moses cried for water. | Exodus 17:4 | God split the rock to bring forth water. |
| People cried out of fear because of the fire God sent. | Numbers 11:2 | God quenched the fire in the camp. |

| Those Who Cried Out | Bible Reference | How God Responded |
|---|---|---|
| Moses recounts the people's cry of hardship in bondage. | Numbers 20:16 | Moses reminds the king of Edom that God sent an angel to bring the people out of bondage in Egypt. |
| There are numerous examples of the people crying out to the Lord. | The times of the judges (Book of Judges) | God heard their cries and provided a deliverer in answer. |
| Samuel cried to the Lord to save the people from the Philistines. | 1 Samuel 7:9–12 | God delivered the people from the Philistines. |

One of the most moving verses revealing God's ability to hear and His desire to intervene through prayer is 2 Samuel 22:4–7:

> I will call upon the LORD, WHO IS WORTHY TO BE PRAISED;
> So shall I be saved from my enemies.
> When the waves of death surrounded me,
> The floods of ungodliness made me afraid.
> The sorrows of Sheol [hell] surrounded me;
> The snares of death confronted me.
> In my distress I called upon the LORD,
> AND CRIED OUT TO MY GOD; HE HEARD MY VOICE FROM
>     HIS TEMPLE,
> AND MY CRY ENTERED HIS EARS.

A person can cry out with his or her voice and never shed a tear. However, when we cry with our voice and weep with our tears, the Lord moves toward those who have a "broken heart, and saves such as have a contrite spirit" (Ps. 34:18). Tears are a physical manifestation of joy, sadness, or brokenness. There is something special about human tears. The fluid that is continually secreted through the eye creates a coating that has numerous chemicals that help fight bacteria. Tears brought about by crying have a slightly different chemical makeup, containing more protein-based hormones; they also have a slightly salty taste, as the liquids in the body contain salt.[10]

The tears flowing down your face eventually reach the corners of your mouth, and the salt can be tasted, reminding a person of the bitterness of their sorrow. But tears also remind us that salt can be used to kill infections in cuts and small wounds. The salty tears are a reminder that weeping endures for a night, but joy comes in the morning (Ps. 30:5). David prayed, "Hear my prayer, O LORD, and give ear to my cry; do not be silent at my tears" (Ps. 39:12).

When King Hezekiah was dying, he sought the Lord for healing, and the Lord instructed Isaiah: "Return and tell Hezekiah the leader of My people, 'Thus says the LORD, the God of David your father: "I have heard your prayer, I have seen your tears; surely I will heal you. On the third day you shall go up to the house of the LORD"'" (2 Kings 20:5). God Himself has a record of your tears, as it is written: "You number my wanderings; put my tears into Your bottle; are they not in Your book?" (Ps. 56:8). The Lord hears the voice of your weeping (Ps. 6:8), and God's compassion moves upon those who weep.

God both *hears* your cries and *sees* your tears. Your weakness must be replaced by His strength. It is Christ who strengthens you (Phil. 4:13). In this passage the word *strengtheneth* (KJV) in Greek is *endunamoo*, meaning empowering. God will renew you in seasons of fainting, when you "wait" upon Him. (See Isaiah 40:31.) Waiting is not sitting in a chair folding your arms. The word *wait* in Isaiah 40:31 means, "to bind together" as twisting threads to weave a garment. Weave your presence into God's presence, and be renewed in your strength.

*Chapter 7*

# WHAT TO DO WITH YOUR BATTERED ARMOR

ONCE A ROMAN SOLDIER ENGAGED IN FACE-TO-FACE combat with arrows flying, spears gashing, and swords slashing, the leather straps, metal strips, and other parts of his armor could become dented and battered. After intense conflict his armor needed repairing. We have been provided a shield of faith. The four Gospels describe different levels of faith:

- *No* faith (Mark 4:40)

- *Little* faith (Matt. 8:26)

- *Great* faith (Matt. 15:28)

- *Such great* faith (Luke 7:9)

In Acts the writer Luke spoke of men like Stephen who were "full of faith" (Acts 6:5, 8). Faith is planted and grows within our hearts. It is obvious, however, that not everyone's faith level is the same as other believers. Four believers with the same request can stand in the front of the elders of a church for prayer (James 5:14). As prayer is offered, the four individuals can have a different reaction—from one of, "I don't know if this will work or not," to "Lord, I hope this works," to "I can't wait to get the next report from the doctor because I know God is taking care of this!"

Some faith shields are thin and flimsy, while others are thick and strong. Engaging in a combination of physical, mental, and spiritual battle at the same time can wear down or impact the shield (faith level). At times I have seen people who were so battered from an extended battle that they literally were in a mode of surrender.

What should we do with battered, dented, or broken armor? Chapter 9 in Isaiah holds a unique verse with a practical application to this question. The prophet Isaiah wrote that the nations in darkness would see a great light, and those living in the shadow of death would come out of (spiritual) darkness (v. 2). He speaks of the rod of the oppressor being broken, along with the yoke of burden (v. 4). He then speaks of the warrior's battle when he writes in Isaiah 9:5 (KJV):

> For every battle of the warrior is with confused noise, and garments rolled in blood; but this shall be with burning and fuel of fire.

The Amplified interprets the verse this way:

> For every [tramping] warrior's war boots and all his armor in the battle tumult and every garment rolled in blood shall be burned as fuel for the fire.

The idea of "confused noise" would refer to the heat of battle, when the shouting, crying, screaming, and sound of horses' hooves and clashing metal fill the air like the rumbling noise of a rocket blasting from its base at a NASA launch site. A warrior must never concentrate on the battle *sounds* but upon the battle *strategy*, not upon the *shouts* of his enemy but on the *spoken instructions* of the Lord of Hosts. When you are engaged in a serious emotional, spiritual, or physical conflict, there will be numerous voices, all giving their own personal advice or warnings, relating their own personal stories, and basically telling you *their secret* to winning *your* battle. Just as Saul's armor would not fit David and David refused to wear what he had not "tested" (1 Sam. 17:38–39), my strategy for victory in my own conflict may not be applicable as your strategy to overcome in the same type of conflict.

I believe there is an important *practical spiritual application* concealed in Isaiah 9:5. What should a believer do when his mind and heart have been battered by countless conflicts, and his armor has been cut with so many holes from the enemies' arrows, spears, and fiery darts that his shield could pass for a target at the shooting range? In Isaiah 9:5 the battered and bloodied armor is *used for fuel in the fire*. Battles are often viewed as a struggle between two forces where one loses and one wins. When it's over, the victor celebrates and enjoys the spoils of war. However, our battles and the beatings we endure should become *the fuel that ignites a burning desire*—a zeal to win the war and move on to the next level of victory.

Years ago the adversary made an attempt to take the life of someone I love very dearly. While watching this person lying on a bed in the emergency room, I knew this was one of the strongest missiles ever sent in my direction, and it took a large shield of faith to cover my spiritual man and defend me from the lying arrows being thrust at my mind. I had to rebuke the spirit of death, the spirit of destruction, and numerous other spiritual entities (Eph. 6:12) that were attempting to cling to my mind and soul and defeat my faith for the life of my beloved friend. I could hear all types of voices trying to plant negative thoughts in my spirit.

At that moment I was in a trial, surrounded by fire (1 Pet. 1:7), and my helmet, breastplate, shield, and even my sword were being tested in the heat of a sudden and unexpected missile strike from the adversary. However, another *fire* rose up in me, and the zeal of the Lord began to burn hot embers of faith inside me like a hot tornado forming out of my inner man. I spoke out loud to the unseen yet very real spiritual enemy behind this assault. I said, "You think you have intimidated me and my friend, but I am going to retaliate against what you have done, and you will regret this as long as I live." At the time I knew my *intention* but not my *mission* to fulfill this statement. However, from that night of trial and after walking through the valley of the shadow of death, a vision came out of the fire with a challenge to raise up a youth ministry and minister to hurting teens, college-age singles, and young adults, bringing deliverance to them through the power of the Holy Spirit. *The dents you see in your armor today from battles in the past should become the fuel for your destiny tomorrow.*

We must learn how to take our most serious trial or strongest temptation and what was intended for our permanent defeat and make it the *fuel of motivation* for ministry. For example, years ago a precious couple saw one of their young children, a beautiful girl under ten years of age, die with a rare disease. They stood in the gap for her healing, but for reasons only known to God the healing never manifested. These were not just *emotional cracks* in their armor—they felt as though the spirit of premature death had burnt their faith to ashes, and their hearts were void of faith and filled with grief.

Someone shared a word with them that just as they were now parents without children, there were many children in the world without parents. Instead of focusing upon their own loss, they must focus upon being parents for those who have no parents—orphans in foreign lands—and raise up their own spiritual children, either in America or on foreign soil. Just as much as they emotionally missed their child, there were children who also missed having a mom and dad. After intensive researching, they became involved in an orphanage and soon discovered that because they ministered to someone else's need, God in return ministered healing to their own wounds. *Their wounds turned to zeal, the zeal into purpose, and the purpose into ministry.*

What about parents who experience the pain of watching a child, perhaps a teenager or a son or daughter in their twenties, die of a drug overdose? Nothing is more heart wrenching than to see a child depart this life prematurely, knowing that God had more for that child but addiction took its toll within his or her body. While you can never bring back that love of your life, there are other parents whose children are presently on the precipice of destruction. You may be the one lifeline, with your financial support of or personal involvement with a rehab center, that pulls them out of drowning in a pool of despair and addiction. Perhaps you can become an addiction counselor, or you can take time to spend with kids who need someone to talk to. *Let the road of your tragedy forge the path for someone else's breakthrough.*

There is a well-respected and highly rated television program called *America's Most Wanted*, which helps track down the worst criminals on the FBI's most wanted list.[1] This program has exposed criminals on the run and assisted in arresting them and bringing them to justice. The motivation for this program came from John Walsh, whose young son was abducted years ago and later found dead. The crushing impact on his armor became the fuel for the fire that motivated this father to make a difference in society and force the passing of special criminal laws that otherwise may have never been passed. One man's sorrow was turned into many other people's joy as criminals in hiding were exposed, judged, and put away through his dedicated work

Believers have protective armor, but unbelievers have no type of protection. While our battles can inspire others toward their own victorious outcomes, the unbeliever is left totally exposed to assaults that lead to their demise or destruction. *What we overcome today becomes our testimony tomorrow, and the dents in our armor drive our determination.*

## Recovering From a Fatal Fall

Since the Roman armor was created by melting metals and forming them in molds, obviously it requires an intensive heat to melt iron ore. From time to time the fiery trials of our faith become so hot that we feel as though we are burning in a furnace heated seven times hotter (Dan. 3:19). If the heat begins to melt the metal and you are consumed and overwhelmed with disaster and defeat, then take the molten metal and re-form a new set of weapons of war to wear. At times the fall of a great man or woman of God requires rebuilding and reconstructing a new armament for recovering from a fatal fall.

When Samson broke his Nazirite vow by telling Delilah the real secret of his strength, God's *champion* was reduced to a *chump*, and the man who took the jawbone of a donkey and slew a thousand Philistines was now blind, bound, and forced round and round in the prison house. (See Judges 16.) His actions were self-invited cracks in his armor. In reality, he simply *didn't have his armor on* when he was sleeping in the lap of Delilah, this charming director of a hair-cutting salon. She began playing with his mind (no *helmet* here), she manipulated his emotions and his heart (no *breastplate* on this guy), yet he kept returning to her house for secret rendezvous. (Where were those *gospel shoes* he should be wearing—Ephesians 6:15?)

The title of Samson's autobiography could have been *When Mighty Men Fall, They Fall Hard.* Samson had broken his Nazirite covenant, causing the Spirit of the Lord to depart from him (Judg. 16:20). For months he served as a human ox, chained to a grinding stone, grinding grain for the Philistines who enjoyed mocking this former Israeli strong man. The enemy, however, ceased to pay attention to one important fact. When a man's hair is cut, in time it will grow back—*just as lost faith can be recovered and restored.* As Samson's hair began to grow, Delilah forgot to keep her scissors close by (v. 22). The enemy assumed that since the Spirit of God had departed, the Lord was finished with this human failure and had exited his life once and for all. Samson felt his hair touching his back and was reminded of his Nazirite vow. (See Numbers 6:2–21.) On one particular day Samson cried out to the Lord two simple words: "Remember me!" The full prayer is in Judges 16:28.

> Then Samson called to the LORD, saying, "O Lord GOD, remember me, I pray! Strengthen me, I pray, just this once, O God, that I may with one blow take vengeance on the Philistines for my two eyes!"

The fatal fall was not fatal after all. The story of Samson is the story of a man of God who forgot to protect himself from his own weakness—a desire for strange women. He could be the businessman who leaves his wife for another woman, or the minister who is bored with ministry and becomes physically involved with a church member, or two youths who go beyond just friendship. Some battles are minor skirmishes leaving bruises, and other wars are life-and-death strangleholds. It is one thing to have a crack in your faith or mind, but it's another thing to leave your armor in the tent and walk out spiritually unprotected, thinking you are Superman or Superwoman and are invincible and beyond falling.

## THE UNPROTECTED MOMENT

There are three primary ways in which spiritual warfare is manifested:

- A sudden, unexpected unguarded moment, like a car that pulls out in front of you or runs a red light

- A strong mental temptation or an event that stretches beyond your time of expectation for deliverance

- A seasonal, repetitious strike of arrows from the adversary that has seasonal gaps of time but repeats itself

On the East Coast, if we hear on the news that an F-4 tornado is within an hour from our town, we have time to prepare. If we are aware that hurricane season has arrived and storms are brewing in the Gulf, those living on the coast prepare for a possible strike and take precautions in advance, not waiting until the wind is tearing the house apart. However, someone else may live on the West Coast in a region that is prone to earthquakes. On three occasions while visiting California, I have experienced three small earthquakes—averaging between 4.5 and 5.2 in intensity. The residents in the state are so used to the mini-quakes, they don't even think about them when the floor of the house is moving! However, according to geological experts, the "Big One" is coming, meaning a large magnitude quake that is linked to the major San Andres fault line running north and south in the Golden State. On the East Coast we can see warnings about the larger hurricanes and tornadoes prior to when they strike, but a major quake comes without warnings. If you are unprepared when the unexpected comes, you may be in the street without water, food, and additional clothing. *In our spiritual struggles we prepare for what we know but get knocked off guard with what we can't see coming.*

We Christians often walk into our local churches with freshly polished armor as though we are in a victory parade and have overcome all spirits, works of the flesh, and spiritual opposition. However, when the sheep depart the fold and are out rubbing shoulders with wolves, at times we hide who we are and compromise while sitting in a restaurant discussing business over the latest alcoholic drinks. Like King Saul, instead of standing against the Goliaths, we hide our armor safely in our tents to prevent anyone from knowing what we are. It is during those *unguarded moments* that the most damage can be done.

Years ago a close friend and I joined together and traveled to Bulgaria shortly after Communism fell. The new freedoms opened doors for the gospel, but they also opened doors for illegal drugs and prostitution. We learned that prostitution ran rampant, and we both stuck together at all times when walking from our rooms to eat or meet the local ministers in the lobby. On this occasion my friend went to the front desk to pay the room charge and check us out while I packed in the room. About fifteen minutes later he came bursting into the room and was praying out loud! I asked, "What happened to you?"

"After paying the bill, I turned to come upstairs and a beautiful woman met me and said, 'Hey American, I can show you a good time,'" he said. "I felt righteous indignation and began to scream back at her, 'Bathsheba, get away from me. You lying devil, get away in Jesus" name!'" He said the woman left quickly, running through the lobby and outside, and he got up here as fast as possible! His reaction reminded me of Joseph when Potiphar's wife attempted to seduce him and he ran out of the palace as fast as possible (Gen. 39:10–13). He had been totally unwarned of what was about to occur but was not unprepared, as his armor went up immediately and his breastplate of righteousness protected him from the smooth words of a harlot.

There have been some ministers and church members who thought, "I am away from people who know me, and no one will ever find out what I'm doing." This type of thinking will cause you to strip off your protective God gear and become open to terrible assaults of the enemy. One of my close missionary friends was with a minister who pastored in the morally wicked city of Amsterdam. One night he was passing out tracts with his church members—all former prostitutes and drug addicts—in a very hard-core, red-light district. They did this as a team and held one another accountable, as all these had come out of this lifestyle and had been won to Christ through personal witnessing. One evening the pastor was stunned to see a well-known American minister (whom I will leave nameless) walk up the street alone and into a building that housed prostitutes. He was not there to "witness" and was in the building for quite some time. It would later be learned that several ministers made occasional trips through Amsterdam and would "visit" certain places during their overnight stays. These *unprotected moments* of greatest vulnerability occur when you willfully choose to lay down your armor, cease to be a soldier for a time, and enter places that are full of land mines and possible spiritual snipers waiting in the dark to take a shot at you.

Samson was the prime biblical example of a man of God who had no business being in the place he was, when he was, with whom he was, and doing what he was doing. He threw his spiritual armor on when he was fighting the Philistines, but he laid it down at the doorstep of Delilah's apartment, picking it back up as he walked out the front door and headed back to the battlefield.

Samson is also a perfect example of God's amazing powerful twins of *mercy* and *grace*. Mercy is God's hand *reaching out* to you, and grace is God's hand *pulling you back* to Himself. Eventually Samson felt his hair tickling the back of his shoulder and heard the echo of the angel's voice that had said, "The child shall be a Nazirite" (Judg. 13:5). When Samson remembered who he was *created to be*, God remembered what He *created him for*—a judge and a deliverer—for God said, "He shall begin to deliver Israel out of the hand of the Philistines" (v. 5). Samson's helmet of salvation suddenly reappeared, and faith was renewed. He knew God could touch him one more time. Thus he cried out, "O Lord God, remember me, I pray...just this once..." (Judg. 16:28).

Samson's comeback was actually a counterattack to avenge his enemies for gouging out his eyes (v. 28). His reviving was so impressive that he slew more enemies in the latter moments of his life than his entire life combined (v. 30). This restoration from a *fatal fall* was so significant in Israel's history that Samson's name is listed in Hebrews among the greatest men of faith in Israel, as a man with faith that pleased God (Heb. 11:32). Recovery is always possible, but humility is required.

Years ago the ministry purchased a Cessna 421 airplane for transporting our team and me to conferences that required a longer distance of travel. The 421 is a piston-engine plane and must be handled properly to prevent messing up the piston engine. I told a ministry friend who had flown a jet about our purchase. He said, "Better bump up to a plane with fuel-injected engines, as your 421 is falling apart every time you start up the engine." A year later I did lose an engine while coming back to Chattanooga from Madisonville, Kentucky, which *inspired me* to bump up to a King Ari F-90, the same type of plane used to fly members of the US military in the United States. The second advice my friend gave me was that when selecting a pilot, I should not just get a *good pilot* but one who had crashed a plane and walked away from it; he is the experienced man!

The same is true with armor. Some women are often looking for a knight in shining armor. Shining armor may be an indicator that he looks good outwardly but may not have battle experience if all he does is sit around and polish his armor! It may be better to find a knight in battered armor—a fellow who has succeeded in getting beat up, engaged in conflict, but still has on his armor with the evidence he has come through some struggles and is still standing. I would rather be a knight in battered armor than a knight in shining armor. The armor is not for public display and bragging rights about who has the shiniest God gear—it is designed to take a "licking and keep on ticking." Let your conflicts be your motivation to do greater things for God.

# Chapter 8

# DISCOVERING and WEARING THE SHIELD of FAVOR

FTER ABRAHAM RETURNED FROM A BATTLE WITH FIVE kings and restored the possessions and people of Sodom to the king of Sodom, God appeared to Abraham and said, "I am your shield, your exceedingly great reward" (Gen. 15:1). In sixteen verses in Psalms, David speaks of a shield, and in fourteen verses of those sixteen, the psalmist speaks of God (the Lord) being his shield (Ps. 3:3; 5:12; 18:35; 28:7; 33:20; 59:11; 84:9, 11; 91:4; 115:9, 10, 11; 119:114; 144:2). As a shield, the Almighty provides divine protection for those who make Him their defense in times of trouble. David certainly needed protection, as he was a warrior from his late teen years when he faced and defeated Goliath. He seemed to be in a battle or family conflict until the latter years of his life, when finally his mighty men refused to let this older soldier go to battle for fear he would be slain by a remaining remnant of giants (2 Sam. 21:17).

There is also another type of shield beside the shield of faith, which David identified in Psalm 5:12: "For You, O LORD, will bless the righteous; with favor You will surround him as with a shield." We have a mental image of favor being a supernatural force, an aura, some unseen vapor from God or some internal charisma pulling people toward some folks like a magnet. We imagine favor as abiding either *in* or *upon* a blessed, righteous person. However, in this passage the psalmist refers to favor as a shield that covers the individual. When you carry a shield of favor, even your enemies will be at peace with you, and what evil is headed in your direction will get aborted before it can ever endanger you.

## THE SHIELDS OF SOLOMON

Years ago in Israel I heard of a Jewish tradition regarding the shields of Solomon that was quite interesting. In the Bible David, Solomon's father, desired to construct the temple of God in Jerusalem. However, the Lord refused his offer, as David was a man of blood and war (1 Chron. 28:3). Solomon succeeded his father, David, as Israel's young king and was known as a man of peace. During his forty-year reign Solomon constructed the most elaborate and expensive temple in world history and made peace treaties with foreign nations, causing Israel to be at the zenith of its prosperity and blessings. We know that Solomon had an army, and he made three hundred gold shields, each containing three pounds of gold, and hung them in the House of the Forest of Lebanon (1 Kings 10:17).

It is said that Solomon placed on each of the shields of his army a special seal called the *Magen David*, or the Shield of David, which we know today as the Star of David—the same six-pointed star emblem found on Israeli flags today.[1] According to Jewish legend this was done by David as a form of protection in the time of battle. In that day most tribes and armies in nations had certain emblems and objects that were considered sacred to their god or religion and that were used in time of battle—certain amulets and emblems that were considered signs of "luck" in crisis or conflict. I have seen people carrying around a rabbit's foot for "good luck." The problem is, *luck* didn't help the rabbit; he lost his foot in the process, so how could the remains of a dead rabbit help a living person?

Unlike the tradition of the shields of Solomon, the believer's shield of favor needs no specific marking or emblem to enhance its strength to protect us, for favor is like a powerful fragrance—you can't see it on the skin, but you can smell it when the person walks into the room. It is like the sun behind the clouds; you can't see the sun itself, but you know that behind the clouds is the warmth of sunlight you are feeling in the air. *Favor is what triggers others to come into agreement with your position and opinion.* Favor is not the door, but it is the hinge on which the door swings open allowing you in the room. Favor marks your place at the table before you ever enter the room. Favor will carry you to places you've never been, seeing things you've never seen and meeting people you have never met who will like you and cannot explain why!

Several years ago a female minister went to the West Coast to minister in the Watts area of Los Angeles—one of the most dangerous parts of the city. These were economically poor areas where specific gangs had marked their turf, and anyone attempting to cross their line was dealt with severely, either through a beating, a drive-by shooting, or an unwanted and unexpected gang attack, often resulting in death. This was one of those times that a ministry police escort was not the way in which to bring the gospel to these inner-city youth. As she began to pray for an open door, she began asking God for favor. God gave her a creative idea that began opening amazing doors in the housing projects. During a very strange turn of events one of the head gang leaders informed her that he was going to serve as her personal bodyguard and that no one in any gang would lay a hand on her. This gang leader actually demanded his followers to help set up the outdoor outreaches and attend the meetings! This was the shield of favor in action. God favored her with protection from the very people who were the most dangerous by giving her favor among enemies.

In the Book of Daniel there were two very dangerous situations that posed threats for Daniel and his Jewish companions. One was when three Hebrew men refused to bow before the king's idol and were cast into a furnace (perhaps the one used to mold the image the king had made to worship) that was heated seven times hotter. (See Daniel 3.) The second narrative was when a den of hungry lions was chomping at the bit for dinner, and Daniel was cast into the den to become the night meal, with his enemies expecting to see lions licking Daniel's bones the following morning. (See Daniel 6.) Daniel escaped without a scratch on his body, and the Hebrew boys came out of the flames without so much as the smell of smoke on their garments. There was a shield of favor protecting each of these four individuals from the destructive plans of men. *God's purpose for them was greater than the enemies' plan against them.* Favor became a fireproof shield and a lion repellent for Daniel and his companions in Babylon.

Back in the late 1980s, prior to one of our main Israel tours, there were uprisings in parts of the West Bank and Gaza among the Palestinian Arabs against the Jews—the *intifada*. At that time Palestinian youths would burn tires in the streets and throw rocks at buses—possibly tour buses that may be passing through some of their villages. On this occasion we were in Jerusalem. Located in east Jerusalem is the Kidron Valley, the ruins of the city of David, the Gihon Springs, Hezekiah's tunnel, and Silwan—an older Arab community with thousands of children and youth living in the houses and apartments on the hillsides. Because of the intifada the Arab schools were closed. I had hoped to take my large tour group through the Kidron Valley, as this region is a very exciting and interesting part of Jerusalem's early biblical history.

My Jewish guides suggested that we avoid this area and cancel the walking tour to prevent any rock-throwing kid from reenacting the biblical story of David and Goliath! When one of my Arab friends heard we were canceling the tour of the area, he said, "Brother, you have God with you, and God's favor. Why would you be fearful? This is God's land, and He wants you to see it." He demanded I take the tour and said, "Let me help you, and don't worry." I had no clue what he meant by that statement, but he said he knew someone who would take care of us. The following day we parked the buses, and as my group of anxious pilgrims began forming, I was met by a husky, rather rugged-looking Arab man in his thirties. He shook my hand and said, "You don't worry about anything. Have a good time."

We took our time walking the entire area with this fellow bringing up the rear. We had no problem, and all of the children simply looked at us and waved their hands; not one picked up as much as a pebble. I later found out that this young man was the brother of one of the biggest Arab leaders among the Palestinians, and everyone knew that if he was with you—then you better not "stir the pot" and cause a stink! I believe this unusual protection was a sign of favor on our tour in the same manner that at times the Roman soldiers would protect Paul from situations that could have brought danger to him.

Another example of favor in the Holy Land was in the early 1980s, where a secret excavation was being conducted under the buildings of the Old City that ran parallel to the Western Wall. At the time it was both secretive and off limits to any visitors, except the archeologists and the Department of Antiquities. My guide, Gideon Shore, introduced me to a Jewish man named Yeshua, who held the keys to all the iron doors, and to one of the head rabbis who was overseeing the underground excavation. The rabbi gave my wife, Pam, and me permission to visit the tunnels late one night, and I was informed that Pam was the first woman to be allowed to visit this area—which was the side where only Orthodox Jewish men were permitted to pray in the tunnels near the Western Wall! For several years on several occasions I received permission to take our entire tour group, late at night, into the tunnels, when it was still off limits for other groups (because of insurance and liability issues). On one occasion the archeologist had changed the locks, and when our group arrived in the night, we were unable to get past the first iron gate leading to the underground site. The rabbi gave an order to have the locks broken for our group to visit. The Jewish guides with me were saying, "This is unheard of. You must have some kind of divine connection with the Lord and the rabbi!"

At times in Israel I have witnessed this favor over and over again. I believe that God's favor is often linked to places and people you love the most. I have a great love for Israel and for both the Arabs and Jews living in the land. This appreciation is visible when each year we air about twenty-five of our *Manna-Fest* television programs that were taped in Israel. People around the world can sense the anointing, joy, and peace of God radiating from the programs. These programs are viewed in 249 nations and countries of the world and among commoners, world leaders, and many from varied religious backgrounds. My sincere love for God's land has opened the door to very prominent Jewish friends, both in Israel and in America. *What and whom you love can forge the strength and size of your shield of favor.*

For a believer favor should be released on a double level: "with God and men" (Luke 2:52). Favor with God is first initiated when we enter into a redemptive covenant though Christ and walk in the commandments and promises of that covenant. When we seek first the success of God's kingdom on earth, then God *adds all things* to us, enabling us to be a successful in what we do (Matt. 6:33).

## FAVOR ON A FOREIGN FIELD

Our VOE organization supports numerous missionaries whom we have personally known and worked with for many years. One in particular, a woman (we will leave nameless), travels into some of the most remote and difficult parts of the world and is assigned by the Holy Spirit to concentrate on people groups who have never heard the gospel. The reason some have never heard is because the physical danger and threats of taking the gospel to these groups is so great that foreign missionaries with children are hesitant to travel and risk their lives. This female missionary must have divine favor from the moment she steps off the plane to the moment she is headed back to America. She tells amazing stories of how God appeared to blind the eyes of border guards to Bibles, protected her from dangerous rebel groups and possible prison time, and the list goes on.

Often when speaking of favor some believe it is just a "Western thing" because we have it easier, and with more churches it means more kingdom connections and financially most Christians have a job or some form of income. However, God's favor is not a regional or ethnic thing; it's a potential blessing for all of the children of God.

One missionary told me about one "underground pastor" (I had seen his picture and heard his testimony) who had been arrested in a Communist nation that persecutes and, at times, tortures Christians. The pastor was placed in a nasty prison cell and was told he would not be fed for ninety days. The soldiers told him that at the end of ninety days they would return to get his rotting carcass out of the prison. The cell was cold, with a dirt floor, and had small holes in the bottom where air filtered in through the night.

Instead of crying and complaining, the minister began thanking God for allowing him to be persecuted for the gospel's sake! He knew he would eventually starve to death in this forsaken place, but he refused to compromise his faith.

He began to praise God, and as he worshipped, he began to think of the story in the Bible where the birds fed the prophet. He looked around and realized there were no windows. He hung his head and became slightly discouraged, and when he did, something caught his attention—a rat had come into his cell and had brought him a fresh apple. He rejoiced, but the miracle didn't end there. The next day the rat brought him a banana. It seemed that the rat was sneaking off with the food of the numerous guards, and he continued to feed him during the ninety days! The water content in the fruit provided enough for his survival.

At the end of ninety days the guards returned expecting to find a stinking corpse, only to find a man who looked healthier than when they put him in the cell—and he was still living! Great fear came upon them as he told them God kept him alive, and they willingly released him from the prison! If ravens, which are an unclean bird, can feed a prophet in a famine in Israel (1 Kings 17:6), why can't a rat (an unclean creature) from a Chinese prison drag in food from enemy soldiers for a suffering minister?

There is often great favor and answers to prayer on the mission field, as these precious believers have no one to turn to except God, and without miracles and supernatural answers to prayer then the impossibilities would remain impossible. I know of an amazing account in Communist China where a minister was arrested and placed in a large refrigerator cooler, left there to die in a short time. In the cooler was also a Communist soldier who had died, his corpse laid there in the cold storage until funeral preparations could be made. The door was shut and locked. In the cooler the Christian began to pray and intercede. Three hours later there was a banging on the door, but it was not the voice of the Christian. The Communist soldier had been raised from the dead, and when the cooler was opened, great fear fell upon the other soldiers, to say the least. These miracles are truly the shield of favor.

Favor is also manifested in the area of ministry travel and business. Years ago one of my coworkers, Robbie James, had taken a small group to India for a mission trip. These trips are very busy, with hours of traveling in vans and numerous meetings throughout the day. By the end of the trip the ministers are quite weary, and the journey home is long and the plane flight usually uncomfortable, to say the least. The Indian pastor prayed that God would favor the group by causing the airlines to upgrade them to business class for their return to America from India where they had been ministering. Arriving at the airport, each upgrade was two thousand dollars, which not only did they not have, but also they would not have paid for if they did have it, as money to missionaries is too precious to spend in that manner. The man at the gate said, "I'll give you five people the upgrade for five hundred dollars each." This too was out of the question. The man went behind the counter and said, "Wait a minute," then returned with five free upgrades for the group at no additional charge. This may seem small, but to five worn-out missionaries it was a much needed refreshing. This was Christian favor in a Hindu nation!

I believe this shield of favor is not only for protection, but also just as the Romans had two shields—one for war and one that was more for beauty—this shield follows with you to open up doors of opportunity that are closed. Faith is not just used in time of a spiritual battle, but faith must also be used on a practical level: believing for a job, believing for income to pay the bills, and believing for good reports and help in practical life situations. There will be times when someone will come to your aid and assistance and will have no explanation as to why he or she helped you—but you will know within yourself, "I am surrounded with the armor of favor."

## BUILDING UP YOUR FAVOR ACCOUNT

Scripture speaks of believers having an "account" in heaven. When Paul received an offering from the church at Philippi, he wrote, "Not that I seek the gift, but I seek the fruit that abounds to your account" (Phil. 4:17). Acts 10:1–4 illustrates how the heavenly blessings are manifested on earth once the heavenly "account" becomes full. The Italian centurion named Cornelius feared God, prayed always, and gave alms (charity) to the poor. When God's angel appeared to him, he revealed, "Cornelius, your prayers and your alms have come up for a memorial before God" (v. 4). The Greek word for "memorial" is *mnemosunon*, which means a reminder or a record. God keeps remarkable records in heaven, including names in the Lamb's Book of Life (Phil. 4:3; Rev. 3:5). Records of the words, deeds, and actions of all men are also recorded in heavenly scrolls (Rev. 20:12–13).

According to Christ, even the smallest deed that is done in His name, including feeding, clothing, and visiting the poor and the prisoner, will not go unrewarded by Him (Matt. 10:41–42). God records the acts and actions of our activities on earth that are done in His name and marks them in His heavenly books for later reference on the Day of Judgment. However, not all rewards are being reserved for handing out from the judgment seat of Christ in heaven (Rev. 11:18). There are certainly various rewards and blessings that are released from God to the earth upon churches and individuals, resulting from a building up and overflow of their heavenly accounts. The church or any individual who continually prays, fasts, witnesses, assists the poor and needy, and performs acts of charity and kindness is recorded in heaven. As we meet the needs of others, God in return meets our needs, releasing blessing for acts of charity and obedience.

My wife and I know of a young woman who, as a young teenager, traveled with her parents, whose job it was to help set up food assistance for the poor during disaster relief efforts. As a young teenager she would help prepare and hand out the food boxes to the poor and elderly. Eventually she became connected with a well-respected youth ministry and worked diligently for years in any and all areas of the ministry where she was asked or needed the most. Years passed, and she was impressed to move to a city where a new ministry was being birthed. There she worked as a volunteer until a door opened for a job. She had spent many years working behind the scenes, serving, helping, and praying continually, often without pay, recognition, or reward. However, at some point her ministry of "helps" (1 Cor. 12:28) caught the Lord's attention. She was in serious need of an automobile and began to seek God for His favor. Without her knowledge, the Lord impressed someone to buy her a vehicle, and not just an old beat-up model, but a very beautiful car. By helping others she had *built up* her favor account in heaven, and God released the *interest* back to her to withdraw from the heavenly *principal* in her account.

## Don't Give Up When the Favor Dries Up

In the days of Elijah a famine was sweeping Israel. A national famine affects both the righteous and the unrighteous. God set up Elijah in a location where there was a brook of flowing water and sent ravens to feed him bread and meat, saying to Elijah, "I have commanded the ravens to feed you" (1 Kings 17:4). Eventually, however, the brook went dry and the birds didn't fly (v. 7). The reason for the sudden drying up of the blessing was because a widow woman and her son were down to their last meal and were going to die, and God needed Elijah to move from his little comfort zone of security and head north toward Lebanon to release a miracle of provision to her life (v. 9).

Life moves in seasons. You cannot always reap, as there comes a season when you must sow to later reap. In Revelation the church at Laodicea was rich and said, "I am rich, have become wealthy, and have need of nothing" (Rev. 3:17). Often, today's believers are constantly trying to become *need less* in the sense of saying, "We need nothing, and all of our needs are always met." The greatest danger to a believer is when he has all he wants, all he needs, and has no needs. Here is why…a needless saint often becomes a prayerless, careless, and useless saint. I have watched people become so comfortable in their prosperity that they see no need to pray, they begin skipping church to enjoy their "stuff," and eventually they become spiritually useless. Needs force you into dependency upon God to provide, thus keeping you on your knees in prayer. I have watched successful businesspeople quit coming to church in order to spend every weekend in a mountain house or on the lake. Suddenly the business or clientele began declining and the "stuff" was sold to pay the bills. They would return to church desiring prayer.

At times the brook goes dry and the birds don't fly, and it seems to you that favor has gone out the front door and left you standing in conflict. When the shield of favor seems to depart, it is time for a self-evaluation.

1. "Am I in some form of sin that is displeasing to God or the Holy Spirit?"

2. "Am I in obedience to the Lord and in His will, or is God getting my attention for a transition I must prepare for?"

Trouble is not a sign of God's disfavor, as trouble is a part of life. However, it should cause us to get alone with God and seek His help.

In my first twenty-five-thousand-square-foot office building (which is still operative) I placed a prayer room in the front for prayer for the needs of people. After several years we ran out of space, and I chose to turn the room into a regular office with a phone secretary. Immediately following my actions, for forty-five days I saw the worst drop in phone orders in the ministry history. It seemed that for hours no one called and ordered any resource material. I became concerned and went to prayer, as we depend upon sales to maintain the VOE ministry in 249 nations. The Lord revealed to me, "Your ministry was built on prayer, and you displeased Me when you removed the prayer room for an office." I responded by turning the room back into the prayer room, where today a sister in the Lord spends the day praying for the needs of the people who call in!

The favor departed as a sign to get my attention to an act of disobedience, but it returned when I followed through with the instruction from the Holy Spirit. For a church and ministry, part of your favor in a community comes from the perception of your ministry within the community. Your personal integrity is part of the shield that makes up your local favor with men and women. By protecting your integrity, you also protect that level of favor. Favor with God comes through obedience to God and His Word. Every believer can enjoy the shield of favor.

If you are a parent and have a child that, let's say, is under the age of ten, and your child comes into the house sincerely crying because he or she fell and has injured the knee, you as a loving, caring parent do not say, "Go sit down, be quiet, and quit whining; I'm busy." A good parent will drop what he or she is doing and tend to the injury, even though it is not life threatening and no medical assistance is needed. The cry of the child releases the love and compassion of the parent.

When the sick, afflicted, and possessed cried out to Christ in the four Gospels, He never rejected one person; instead He stopped, prayed, and ministered. When we cry out to our heavenly Father, He immediately hears us, as David said in Psalm 120:1: "In my distress I cried to the LORD, and He heard me." *For God to reach down to you, you must first reach up to Him. Prayers are released through words, but compassion is released through tears,* and Christ is moved with compassion toward your needs (Matt. 9:36; 14:14; 20:34).

# Chapter 9

## MENDING CRACKS in
## a BROKEN VESSEL

Most people in North America are familiar with pottery. Biblical pottery was made of stone but primarily of clay, which was fashioned by the hands of a master potter, then fired at high temperatures to harden the vessel for public usage. During the firing process the clay undergoes a chemical change, which hardens the soft clay into a permanently shaped container. In 1 Kings 7:46 King Solomon ordered that the temple vessels be cast from clay molds from the area of Succoth and Zaretan. According to Jewish sources, these vessels were made out of clay molds formed from the wet clay found in the Jordan River. Many of the sacred vessels used in the temple service were made of gold or silver and others cut from stone. Each temple vessel served a distinct purpose and was considered holy in the eyes of both God and the priest.

In the Old Testament the Hebrew word *keliy* can be translated in the Bible as "vessel" (Lev. 6:28), "bag" (1 Sam. 17:40), and "instrument" (Isa. 54:16). Vessels were acquired to store and transport such resources as water, oil, grains, or fruit. Vessels could be found in local homes, on farms, and near wells of water and were necessary on a daily basis.

At the beginning of Creation God is depicted as a potter forming man from the clay of the earth into a human vessel made in God's image (Gen. 2:7). Throughout the Old Testament the inspired writers would allude to God as the Master Potter, molding Israel, the Hebrew people, and the nations for His divine purposes (Isa. 29:16; 64:8; Jer. 18:1–6). As God is shaping the pottery in its early stages on His potter's wheel, at times it becomes marred or flawed, and the Master Potter must crush the wet clay and begin all over.

> And the vessel that he made of clay was marred in the hand of the potter; so he made it again into another vessel, as it seemed good to the potter to make.
> —JEREMIAH 18:4

Throughout the Bible there are seven different types of vessels, and all seven paint the imagery of the seven types of individuals that God deals with. The seven types of vessels mentioned in the Bible are:

1. The earthen vessel

> But the earthen vessel in which it is boiled shall be broken. And if it is boiled in a bronze pot, it shall be both scoured and rinsed in water.
> —LEVITICUS 6:28

2. The vessels of honor

> Does not the potter have power over the clay, from the same lump to make one vessel for honor and another for dishonor?
> —ROMANS 9:21

3. The vessels of dishonor. The reference to the vessel of dishonor is also found in the above passage, Romans 9:21:

Does not the potter have power over the clay, from the same lump to make one vessel for honor and another for dishonor?

4. The vessels of wrath

What if God, wanting to show His wrath and to make His power known, endured with much longsuffering the vessels of wrath prepared for destruction?

—ROMANS 9:22

5. The chosen vessels

But the Lord said to him, "Go, for he is a chosen vessel of Mine to bear My name before Gentiles, kings, and the children of Israel. For I will show him how many things he must suffer for My name's sake."

—ACTS 9:15–16

6. The broken vessels

I am forgotten like a dead man, out of mind;
I am like a broken vessel.

—PSALM 31:12

7. The vessels of mercy

And that He might make known the riches of His glory on the vessels of mercy, which He had prepared beforehand for glory.

—ROMANS 9:23

These seven vessels identify the seven spiritual characteristics found in each person and how God views each person based upon the level of their spiritual walk.

- *The earthen vessel:* We are all earthen vessels formed from the clay of the earth by the Master Potter. As vessels of clay, we are subject to being broken if mishandled or mistreated or if internal pressure builds, making a weak spot on our vessel, which eventually causes a small crack.

- *The vessel of honor:* This is any vessel who will submit to God's will and purpose, following Him through obedience in every area of his or her life. The life and work of such an individual bring honor to the Lord and to His name.

- *The vessel of dishonor:* This is any vessel intent upon continuing a life in sin, following the pleasures of this world and in disobedience to God and His Word.

- *The vessel of wrath:* These are those who commit the sin of blasphemy or live in sins of perversion to the point they are given over to a reprobate mind (Rom. 1:28). These are vessels assigned to experience the wrath of God and would include Judas and the future Antichrist.

- *The broken vessel:* These are the earthen vessels who have faced negative circumstances in their lives and have experienced what we term "a broken heart" or have had an experience that has brought grief and sorrow to their lives.

- *The chosen vessel:* The chosen vessel is the vessel or person whom God chooses from birth for a specific assignment in the nation or in the kingdom. The prophet Jeremiah was a chosen vessel from before his birth (Jer. 1:5), and Paul was also identified as a chosen vessel (Acts 9:15).

- *The vessel of mercy:* As God's grace is poured out upon our lives and we live in spiritual freedom from the sins and bondages of the past, we are marked as vessels of mercy who are able to give mercy to others as we have also received mercy.

Since this book is dealing with cracks in a believer's armor, in this section I want to focus on one of these vessels, the broken vessel, and reveal how to seal the cracks in an earthen, broken vessel to bring a wholeness to where the weakness has been.

### RESTORING THE BROKEN VESSEL

Having been to Israel more than thirty-four times, I have stood on what is called a *tel*—a mountain or hill that rises in a valley where an ancient town or city was built. When the archeologist begins to unearth the ruins, it is common to find thousands of shards, which are pieces of broken clay pottery. At times an entire pot has lain under the dirt in one place for thousands of years. Because cities were often the target of invading armies, few clay vessels survived the collapse of the homes or the roofs that fell after being burned. A keen archeologist, however, can mark each piece of broken pottery and glue the pot back together. The only negative is that you can visibly see all the broken pieces that resemble a clay puzzle, identifying that this vessel was totally broken and is now glued back together.

There are many believers who have had to *pick up the pieces* of a broken life—such as a broken marriage, trying to split assets, figure out visiting rights and child support, and move from one job or home to a new location. While many believers continue to follow the Lord despite the brokenness, their eyes, facial expression, talk, and actions reveal they are living one day at a time, or *one piece at a time*, trying to find some order in a season of disorder.

However, there are other forms of pottery, even in Christ's time, that would have just one crack that would appear or a small section that needed repairing. The ancient process of restoring a cracked vessel is one of the most remarkable pictures of how the Lord restored the broken vessels in the house of the potter.

## A CRACK IN THE VESSEL

The more valuable vessels were created with molds using silver or gold. It requires intensive heat to melt the silver and gold found in the earth, to purify the metals from the dross, or natural impurities mixed with the ore or gold taken from the earth. Pure silver melts at 1,761 degrees Fahrenheit; to melt gold (24 karat) requires a heat of about 1,945 degrees Fahrenheit.[1] Proverbs speaks of removing the dross:

> Take away the dross from the silver, and there shall come forth a vessel for the finer.
> —PROVERBS 25:4, KJV

Scripture speaks of certain trials of our faith being fiery trials that are as precious as gold being purged in the fire (1 Pet. 1:7). Peter was writing to believers who were in heaviness through manifold temptations (v. 6). The dross is always mixed in with the pure metal, but it must be separated to place the melted silver and gold in molds or in the hands of a refiner who can forge a valuable container. It is the dross that makes a believer unclean in his or her spirit.

God gave instruction through Moses concerning the laws of clean and unclean vessels. What was placed inside of the vessel could contaminate the sanctity of the vessel, including forms of mildew. If a dead reptile fell into a vessel, the vessel was unclean and must be cleansed with water (Lev. 11:32). If a person with a sore or a bodily discharge handled a vessel, the wooden vessel could be cleaned with running water, but the earthen vessel was broken (Lev. 15:12). If a man died in his tent, any vessel that was open without a lid covering was considered unclean (Num. 19:14–15).

God knew that all germs and many diseases are airborne and could cause a person to become contagious by contracting that particular germ or airborne virus. Germs are also invisible, and what you don't see that gets inside your vessel can cause as much damage as what you do see! When vessels were classified unclean, they were either unclean until the evening or unclean for seven days. Many times fellow believers will observe the outward actions or appearance of other followers of Christ and prejudge their weakness or strengths based upon words and actions. However, some of the worst defilement of the human spirit comes from attitudes and internal struggles that are effectively hidden from eyes. As Paul wrote, "Looking diligently lest anyone fall short of the grace of God; lest any root of bitterness springing up cause trouble, and by this many become defiled" (Heb. 12:15), and "To the pure all things are pure, but to those who are defiled and unbelieving nothing is pure; but even their mind and conscience are defiled" (Titus 1:15–16). It is unforgiveness, bitterness, strife, envy, and malice that defile the vessel internally.

## THE FORMATION PROCESS

God has placed His treasure in earthen vessels (2 Cor. 4:7). Earthen vessels were formed from clay taken from the earth, just as the first man, Adam, was created from the ground (Gen. 2:7). Clay at times can become so dry that it becomes unworkable and will not bend under the hand of the maker; at times believers can experience spiritual dry spells in which they cease to grow or mature. Just like the children of Israel in the wilderness, they are camped in one place, bored with the routine, or going in circles around the same mountain over and over. If the dry spells do not impact them, then their spiritual balance may be the next area where their development is hindered.

When the clay is on the potter's wheel, the formation can actually get off balance, off center, and out of shape, causing the potter to have no other choice but to crush the clay and begin reforming another vessel from the same clay. I have seen this when believers fall into a sin, leave church, and return. They must lay again a foundation of good works and do their first works over (Rev. 2:5).

A third area in the formation process on the potter's wheel is when small stones are mixed in with the clay, or hard lumps appear in the walls of the future vessel. These must be removed, or during the firing process when the clay is being heated for final hardening and public service, the heat can cause the vessel to have a place of weakness, which could make the vessel unusable when it is placed in use. I view these small stones as the "weight, and the sin" that Hebrews 12:1 says can easily ensnare us or weigh us down and cause us to slow our pace in the race.

Vessels can also be marred, and these are a picture of the character flaws in a person's life. They are many younger believers who desire to be used of God in a public setting—such as a worship leader, teacher, pastor, youth minister, missionary, and so forth. However, they are marred or have flaws and rough edges they must work on before being placed in a public setting. I know of at least one minister of music who was fresh out of four years of college with a degree and was hired as music minister at a church with a large church choir. In one year's time the choir went from seventy-five members to twenty and almost caused a split in the church. The young man was a novice, lifted up in pride, and he refused to communicate with the choir members properly. He passed the grade with his book knowledge but failed the grade with his practical knowledge. This is why Paul warned that you must be careful placing a novice (a newly planted believer) in an important position within the church, as he or she can become lifted up in pride (1 Tim. 3:6).

When David was at the lowest point of his life as a result of his sins, he wrote, "I am forgotten like a dead man, out of mind; I have like a broken vessel" (Ps. 31:12). Any object made of clay or glass can be broken. Glass can crack if the temperature moves from one extreme to another. Clay vessels can crack by being dropped or mishandled or by having a weak spot in one area. In ancient times clay vessels were used by all nationalities of people. Clay vessels were strong unless they were put under extreme pressure, dropped, or cracked. Every person at some point of time will encounter a crack in his or her attitude, thought life, spiritual walk, or in dealing with others. *These are the cracks in our armor.* When these cracks occur in our attitude, we will begin thinking thoughts that we would normally avoid. Eventually the cracks are like an untreated cut; they form a spiritual infection that sets in, and soon we are not the same person we were. The negative thoughts in our head have taken the eighteen-inch drop from the mind to our heart.

Once a vessel is cracked, it cannot effectively hold its liquid contents. It ceases to be what it was created to be. If it was created to hold water, then water will leak from the crack. If it held oil, then oil will flow out of the small opening. A cracked vessel can be filled to the brim; however, if it is cracked, in just a few moments the precious liquid will form a puddle on the outside of the vessel.

## LEAKY BELIEVERS

There is what I call *leaky believers.* They can receive a spiritual blessing in an altar service, and before they arrive home, the peace and joy of their blessing have lifted. They receive an infusion of the joy of the Lord on Wednesday night, only to have the smile and glow on their countenance become a frown and a dull expression by Thursday morning. As an illustration, they are like the huge house with five bathrooms. In the morning everyone is in the shower at the same time getting ready for work or school. Within minutes all the hot water is gone. It was not because there was a *shortage* of hot water but because the hot water was forced through too many pipes at one time!

Believers who were wounded in their emotions or in their spirits by hateful words, negative past experiences, or physical abuse are often stuck in a pit of the past, chained with the bands of unforgiveness, and are often challenged with the ability to remain steadfast and stable, not living in the cracks. I have actually observed believers wounded from past experiences who were unable to properly function throughout a normal day. Certain people, words, or actions were like a trigger on a gun that caused the believer to "go off" into an unexpected rant and rave, causing embarrassment to the believer and discomfort to his or her colleagues. One day they are Dr. Jekyll, and the next, Mr. Hyde!

I have actually seen believers who are so cracked in their emotions that when they come to work, their coworkers don't know if they are going to experience Dr. Jekyll or Mr. Hyde! One day they act as if they have been to a resurrection, and the following day as if they have just returned from a funeral. The worst crack comes from those who have fallen into sin.

## BELIEVERS WITH CRACKED BONES

There is no greater example in the Bible of a person who truly loved God and was consumed with His presence, but who fell from the height of God's glory to the pit of despair, than King David. David was a singer and a harp player whose gift was so anointed that he would play a harp and evil spirits would depart from Saul (1 Sam. 16:16). As a teenager, David killed a giant whom for forty days no other Israeli soldier would battle (1 Sam. 17). After becoming king, David constructed a tent for continual worship and brought the ark of the covenant to Jerusalem and placed it in this tabernacle—the place where many of the psalms were written (1 Chron. 15–16). However, David had one dark side. He committed adultery with another man's wife, she became pregnant, and David had the husband set up to be killed in battle (2 Sam. 11–12).

After David's sin was exposed, he was viewed in a totally different way by his peers and the people in his kingdom. He lost the joy of salvation and began to feel the presence of the Lord leak out of his own soul, leaving him with a feeling of anguish and despair. At one point David cried out to God:

> Let me hear joy and gladness;
>> let the bones you have crushed rejoice.
> Hide your face from my sins
>> and blot out all my iniquity.
>> —PSALM 51:8–9, NIV

It is easy to stand up in church with your hands raised in a worship atmosphere, shout an occasional amen to the preacher, and rejoice with the praise and worship band when the people around you are ignorant and uninformed about your past. It is quite different when you have fallen into sin and the entire church, community, state, and nation know the details! Even after you have publicly repented, some people may look at you and say, "Who does he think he is...the old hypocrite? How can she act like this in church after what she did?" The reason fallen people get up and get their rejoicing back is because they have learned David's secret—*how to dance with broken bones.*

## DAVID THE DANCING KING

From the time of a youth David loved worship. One cannot read the Psalms without seeing his passion for worshipping his King.

One of David's most notable moments was when he brought the ark of the covenant to the Jerusalem, the city of David.

In 2 Samuel 6 David had prepared a huge processional from the house of Obed-Edom to Mount Zion, where David had erected a tent to house the precious ark. As the Levites carried the ark on their shoulders, David offered sacrifices every six paces (v. 13). The distance from Obed-Edom's house to Jerusalem was an estimated eighteen miles. This means there was an eighteen-mile trail of sacrificial blood behind this worshipping processional! The spiritual principle is this: *it requires the blood of Christ to cover your past!* You can't progress in your future unless your past has been hidden in the blood of Christ! Once the blood is applied, the adversary cannot sneak up behind you and bring up what has been covered in the blood of Christ.

Once David arrived at the gates of Zion, he began dancing before the Lord with "all of his might." His wife, who was in the palace watching from a window, became angry with the king. She later accused him of showing off for the young women who were present in the crowd (vv. 16–21). David's wife was Michal, Saul's daughter. Her father was so spiritually out of touch with God's presence in his day that the glory of the Lord had departed from Israel and the enemies of Israel were wreaking havoc on the nation, which was in debt, discontent, and distress (1 Sam. 22:2). David refused to be intimidated by his wife and her criticism of his worship.

The incident brought stress on their marital relationship. Apparently David refused to have any relationship with her, because the Bible says that she "had no children to the day of her death" (2 Sam. 6:23). Just as she became barren and unfruitful because of her criticism of true worship, so today's believers need to beware of becoming opinionated and verbally critical of the worship of the younger generation or of being judgmental of their music or appearance. Those who criticize spiritual truth in any form face the possibility of their own spiritual impotence and fruitlessness. David loved to worship and to dance. However, the affair with Bathsheba, the murder of her husband, and the death of Bathsheba's son was overwhelming to David. He had lost his joy and his desire to worship.

## BAD BONES AND LIMPING WORSHIP

After David's secret sin was publicly exposed, how could this fallen warrior, who could deliver himself from the paws of a lion but not from the arms of a woman, ever worship before his people again? Throughout the cobblestone street corners, the shops, and the homes the name *David* was now synonymous with *adulterer* and *murderer*. When David stepped out on the balcony of his palace, people would smirk. Close friends were keeping a distance, and others perhaps spoke of a new king. To worship a righteous God after demonstrating unrighteous actions tagged the king as a hypocrite. David understood his fall and also God's mercy. This is why he looked heavenward seeking forgiveness and repenting of his iniquity. He cried out to God so that his broken bones would again be able to rejoice. Two important truths should be elaborated on here:

1. David knew his *bones* were spiritually broken and there would always be a *limp* as a result of his sin. The writer of Proverbs speaks about adultery and says it brings "wounds and dishonor," and the "reproach will not be wiped away" (Prov. 6:33). The man writing these words was Solomon, the son of Bathsheba. Perhaps while growing up Solomon had heard his mother, Bathsheba, and his biological father, David, speak about how their choices had caused division,

discouragement, disillusion, and great embarrassment to the people of Israel. David knew he would always bear some type of a *limp* in the eyes of the people.

2. David also recognized that it was in the Lord's power to restore his joy and to allow the bones to rejoice again. The Hebrew word for "rejoice" is *giyl*, which comes from a root word meaning, "to spin around under the influence of a violent emotion." It doesn't just mean to be happy, to clap your hands, or to smile and say, "Praise the Lord." It alludes to dancing and rejoicing in a very emotional manner.

At the time of David's failure, he could have presented numerous requests to the Lord. He could have requested, "Please restore my reputation as king," or, "Please restore my integrity in the eyes of the people." Had David been an American politician, he could have hired a Hollywood agency to make his sin appear to be a "right-wing conspiracy" or place the blame on his Secret Service agents for allowing this woman in the palace. He could have taken polls to determine how to manipulate the story for best damage control. Within a year the Washington spin doctors could have made Bathsheba look like a stalker and the king an innocent victim of a wild woman's fantasy.

David, however, didn't play games with God's mercy. He knew he had sinned and knew everyone else knew. He simply looked up and asked God that his joy be restored (Ps. 51:12). He wanted to take God dancing again! He missed those intimate moments he and his heavenly Father had enjoyed, beginning in his teen years. Sin had caused the divine presence to depart from him just as the air conditioner's cool air disappears when the power goes out. There was no spiritual refreshing. The lust of the flesh and lust of the eyes had split David's spiritual armor, opening his heart to unspeakable thoughts and breeding images that turned into actions. *And all David wanted was to dance with broken bones!*

## GETTING YOUR DANCE BACK

There are numerous psalms called the "psalms of repentance," where David is remembering his sins and calling out to God for mercy and forgiveness. In Psalm 51 David is crying out to God, "Let my broken bones dance again!" As the years passed, toward the end of his life, David began to reemphasize worship, and in Psalm 150 he pens, "Let everything that has breath praise the LORD" (v. 6). David lists numerous musical instruments and instructed the players to praise God with their instruments. In verse 4 of this psalm he instructs, "Praise him with the…dance!" The wounded king with broken bones was restored to the point he took back his worship, and once again he danced before the Lord prior to his departure.

There are several types of wounds but basically two ways of getting them: uninvited wounds and self-inflicted wounds. The uninvited are initiated by outside forces or circumstances over which you have no control. You had no control over your boss laying you off from work, your husband leaving you for an old girlfriend, or your parents divorcing. However, at times our choices become a sword that turns on us, and we are wounded by self-inflicted cuts from our own decisions. When your vessel is broken, you will tend to withdraw and pull yourself away from other vessels that seem flawless and have never cracked under pressure. However, cracks in the vessel are opportunities for grace and mercy to take you dancing!

## DANCING WITH MERCY AND GRACE

You can rejoice and dance with broken bones because mercy and grace are your dancing partners. Mercy whispers, "The master is waiting for you to meet Him in the secret place again. He has missed you." Grace begins to reach down and pick you up, promising, "Come on; I can place you in His arms again." The mercy of God and the grace of God make you worthy to rejoice, even after you have failed. Forgiveness is more than an act—it is a fact.

I have often said that we really do not understand the length and breadth of God's mercy and forgiveness. If we were in charge of humanity, Noah's life after the Flood would have been expunged from the biblical record for planting a vineyard and getting drunk and lying around naked (Gen. 9:21). The next narrative would be to remove Lot, the father who today could have been arrested for having relations with his own daughters (Gen. 19:31–38). David would have been impeached as king for his adultery with Bathsheba (2 Sam. 11). The apostle Peter would have had his ministerial license revoked by denominational hierarchy for publicly denying the Lord (Mark 14:71).

When Peter asked Jesus, "How often shall my brother sin against me, and I forgive him? Up to seven times?" (Matt. 18:21), Peter limited his forgiveness to seven times. Jesus replied, "I do not say to you, up to seven times, but up to seventy times seven" (v. 22). Jesus was saying that as long as the offender asked the offended person for forgiveness, it should be given to him, indicating that the release of forgiveness is to be unlimited.

Many years ago I heard my close friend, Dr. E. L. Terry, explain the various vessels in the Bible, and what, in ancient times, the owner of a cracked clay vessel could do to mend it. When a clay jar was cracked, there were two main substances needed to seal the crack: fresh wet clay and the blood of a special tick. If wet clay was inserted in or on the crack and it dried, there was nothing to hold the fresh dried clay onto the older vessel once it dried. Thus pressure from any internal liquid could push the new seal out, and the pot would return to its previous condition. A tick is an insect that sucks blood from animals such as dogs, cats, sheep, goats, horses, and even humans if they can attach their heads under the skin. When a tick is crushed, small amounts of blood are released.

The particular tick used for this process was taken from a sheep or a goat. The blood of the tick was mixed with the wet clay, and the combination of the clay and the blood allowed the clay to dry and hold on to the edges around the crack. Thus the blood was needed to create the seal to hold the fresh clay in place.

The application is very clear. We are human beings with passion, affections, and emotions subject to weakness, hindrances, frustrations, and outright assaults that continually beat against our armor. As humans we are made from the clay (dust) of the earth and will return to dust. If we attempt to heal wounds and seal unwanted openings with clay methods or human ideas, our actions may sustain us for a season, but the next wave of pressure beating against our vessel will cause the weakness to reappear. Just as the blood of a tick on clay can assist in filling the cracked gap, the blood of Christ not only redeems (1 Pet. 1:19) but also forgives (Eph. 1:7) and removes the shame and guilt of a broken vessel! *It is possible to still dance with broken bones!*

# *Chapter 10*

# DON'T GO TO HELL
# OVER A MYSTERY!

I WANT TO TELL YOU ABOUT MY FATHER, FRED STONE, A MAN OF great faith and dedication to Christ, who ministered for more than sixty-one years before his death in March of 2011. My first memories of Dad are when he pastored a small church in the rural community of Big Stone Gap, Virginia. From the simple age of five to my mature age of fifty-one, in my eyes Dad always seemed strong, in charge, confident of God's ability, and keenly sensitive to knowing God's will for himself and others. In his last ten years of life he traveled and ministered in churches. Observers and partners of his ministry often spoke of Dad's strong compassion for the sick and afflicted. Spending hours a day in prayer, he ministered at night in churches or conventions. It was common to see him in front of a large line of people seeking prayer, often accompanied by outbursts of sudden praise to God for an instant healing of some form. He saw numerous people healed of cancer. Yet Dad passed away with kidney failure from diabetes, unable to drink or eat for about ten days until his body gave up and released his spirit to God.

Herein lays a perplexing enigma. How can a man who has prayed the prayer of faith for so many individuals who were suffering and diseased, and who were healed through his prayers, yet pass away with a sickness? Dad and I both discussed this before his passing. It was pointed out that when Isaac was old, his "eyes were dim" (Gen. 27:1, KJV) and he had difficulty telling his two sons, Jacob and Esau, from one another. By touching their arms and hearing their voices he was able to distinguish between the two (vv. 21–22). Elisha received a double portion of the anointing and Spirit that was on Elijah (2 Kings 2). Scholars note that Elijah performed sixteen miracles; however, Elisha experienced thirty-two, which is double the miracles of his teacher, Elijah.[1] Toward the conclusion of Elisha's life we read, "Elisha had become sick with the illness of which he would die" (2 Kings 13:14).

What makes this statement even more confounding is that after Elisha died, during a battle a dead soldier was thrown into the burial crypt of Elisha, and the dead man revived when he touched Elisha's bones (vv. 20–21). With this level of God's power within the bones of this dead prophet, why would, or better yet, how could any form of sickness attach itself to this mighty man of God? Would not the resurrection power within his body attack any sickness in his body? In the New Testament we are aware that Christ went about "healing all who were oppressed by the devil" (Acts 10:38). Yet within the early church were men who themselves needed a physical healing manifestation. We read where Paul wrote that Epaphroditus "was sick almost unto death; but God had mercy on him, and not only on him but on me also, lest I should have sorrow" (Phil. 2:27). Paul said of another of his companions in ministry, "Trophimus I have left in Miletus sick" (2 Tim. 4:20). Even young Timothy was agonizing with stomach problems; Paul said Timothy had "infirmities" (1 Tim. 5:23). The Greek word for "infirmities" is *astheneia* and refers to a weakness from a sickness or some form of a physical sickness.

The fact is that eventually all men will die, usually through three common methods: old age, sickness, or an accident. Because we live on a planet that is presently under a sin curse, the human body is subject to bacteria, parasites, flus, and at times diseases. The weakening of the body can be a source for certain sickness within the body, as the immune system is compromised with time and age. A believer passing with a sickness is no indication of any form of sin or disobedience in his or her life, as some may teach. It is a law of life that says, "It is appointed for men to die once" (Heb. 9:27).

In my father's situation, he had diabetes and, in reality, did not take care of himself as he should. To prevent offending someone in the mountains of Kentucky or West Virginia, he would eat the high-starch and high-carb foods and even sweets. When a piece of cake or pie found its way on his plate, he *ate what was set before him*, in respect for the cook. Only in the latter years did he change his diet, but the damage was already done to the internal organs.

At times you will have a very godly person who believes in prayer, healing, and miracles who will pass away suddenly through an accident or a disease. The church will pray and believe, and yet the individual being prayed for will see no change and will move to his or her eternal destination. In some cases, this situation of praying yet not receiving puts a *huge crack* in the shield of faith for some people. Instead of thanking God for the person and knowing they will see him or her again in heaven, they begin to question God's ability and willingness to heal or to answer a healing prayer in the future.

This is a serious issue with some. I suggest that you should never change your biblical theology to accommodate a tragedy. My father once said, "When I pass, tell people I still believe in a God who heals the sick!" Dad never changed his theology of healing, even though his own body never experienced a full recovery. To him, he lived a full life, ministered for more than sixty-one years, passing at age seventy-eight, and was ready to go home and enter into his eternal rest! Even Scripture teaches that a man can be given seventy years and, by reason of strength, eighty (Ps. 90:10). We must be thankful for the many good years and not disqualify our faith for the closing years of a physical crisis when crossing the finish line.

What happens, however, when the death is not an older person who we know is going to pass anyway but is an infant who passes in a crib at home, or a child in a deadly accident, or a mom who passes with cancer, leaving three small children and a father who dies while working on the job? These early departures from life often cause survivors to question God's *goodness*, His love, and even His *existence*. Without some spiritual understanding, they will throw away the anchor of their faith, causing a spiritual shipwreck as they are unable to maneuver through the fog of questions veiling their understanding.

## THE CHARLES GREENAWAY STORY

One of the most remarkable stories I have ever heard concerning how God can take a terrible situation and turn it around is the story of Charles Greenaway. Charles Greenaway was an ordained minister in the Assemblies of God in the 1930s in Elba, Alabama. Deep within he had a desire to travel to the mission fields and serve as a missionary. There was one thing preventing this burden for mission from being fulfilled—his son, Daniel.

You see, Daniel was a beautiful child, but he had contacted leukemia. The Assembly of God missions could not risk a minister living overseas in a foreign nation with such a sick child, as there would be few if any treatments and the suffering fellow would consume the time of his father and mother. The Greenaways submitted to the decision and remained in America, where Charles continued to pastor while his son received treatment for the leukemia. In his older years Charles told a missionary friend of mine that on one occasion their car had broken down and there were four old, bald-treaded tires on the vehicle. It was hot outside, and his wife was in the car with Daniel. A minister they knew drove by, and instead of helping them, he beeped his horn and went on his way.

Charles believed that God was certainly able to heal his son, and often he and others prayed for this to occur. Despite the prayers, Daniel's condition worsened, and eventually his suffering became so great that his wife told her husband that she didn't want to see the lad suffer any more and asked that he pray that the Lord would come and take their son to heaven to be with Him. After prayer, at age nine, Daniel slipped into eternity, where his soul and spirit met the Savior and he was at rest with the Lord.

Immediately after Daniel's departure, Charles prayed a prayer, which, once I was told the words, I have never forgotten. He thanked the Lord for giving him Daniel and noted to God that he did not understand why Daniel was not healed, but he told God: *"I will not go to hell over a mystery!"* He was saying that he did not understand the ways of God, the reason why his prayer was unanswered, and why his son passed at age nine. However, he refused to lose his faith, trust, and confidence in the Lord, despite the fact he was in sorrow and grief losing his son.

The story does not end there. After the death of Daniel, Charles reapplied for a position on the mission field and was accepted. During his long and illustrious ministry he and his wife had two children born on the field. Greenaway started seventeen thousand churches, thirteen Bible colleges, and preached on every continent of the world except Antarctica. One man touched the entire world because he refused to allow a large crack to divide his faith and make him question the purposes of God!

## MAD AT GOD

Events on earth that cause destruction and death are often blamed on God for either *causing* them or for *not preventing* them. Men seem to forget that while God did create the earth and all living things, He originally gave man "dominion" over the creation (Gen. 1:26–27). Man's dominion includes control over the atmosphere, the land, sea, and the animal kingdom. It is obvious that man has done a terrible job in being the steward of the planet and caring for his earthly inheritance, handed to man in the Garden of Eden! Multitudes starve, and blood fills the streets when evil men rise up as dictators, bringing a spirit of death and destruction with them.

One example of God being blamed for not preventing a tragedy was the Holocaust. For those unfamiliar with the event, Adolf Hitler arrested millions of Jews throughout Europe, sending them to death camps and gas chambers and eliminating an estimated six million Jews—including one and a half million children who also perished in the most terrible and violent manner. When the world saw the pictures, they were horrified and unable to imagine how a loving God could permit an ethnic group He identifies as His "chosen people" to experience such horrific experiences.

Among those who survived the Holocaust and eventually immigrated to Israel or moved to other parts of Europe are those who became atheists and agnostics, as they could not imagine a God who would permit such suffering. The internal struggle led to theological minds debating the goodness of God. Just how *in charge* was God in the affairs of men? There was also a strong animosity birthed in the hearts of many survivors who placed blame on some people in Europe, who called themselves Christians, for not standing up and defending the Jewish people in the greatest crisis of their history. Many secular or nonreligious Jews were and are unaware that in the first five books of the Bible written by Moses (called the Torah), the Hebrew prophet Moses foresaw a time eerily parallel to the Holocaust in which he warned the Jewish people what would come in the future. But he also gave them hope that God would deliver them and restore them to their land and position as a nation among the nations. All of what Moses wrote concerning the death, destruction, and the restoration has come to pass. (See Deuteronomy 28.)

The anger toward the Almighty is also found in the Gentile nations. Several years ago, when the tsunami struck Indonesia, there were hundreds of thousands of deaths, including the deaths of thousands of children. Since the Book of Genesis indicates that God created the heavens and the earth, including the sea and all living things therein (Gen. 1), the assumption is that God is controlling all natural disasters, including earthquakes, storms, and tsunamis. Those believing this immediately announced that the judgment of God had fallen upon certain nations since these natural disasters are often labeled by insurance companies as "acts of God." Thus God is to blame for the event and the resulting deaths and destruction.

Consider earthquakes for a moment. When Moses was upon Mount Sinai, the mountain trembled as a result of God's presence (Ps. 68:8). However, when Elijah stood upon Mount Horeb, the mountain shook with an earthquake, but we read: "...but the LORD was not in the earthquake" (1 Kings 19:11). On one mountain God is shaking the rocks, and on another mountain the hill is shaking and the Lord has nothing to do with it.

Then, hundreds of years later, Paul and Silas were singing praises to the Lord, and God sent an earthquake that rocked a prison, causing the metal bars to burst open and all the prisoners to go free. No one was injured or killed in this quake (Acts 16:25–26).

When Christ was riding a boat on the Sea of Galilee, a storm called a "tempest" struck, covering the boat with water (Matt. 8:24). The Greek word for "tempest" is *seismos* and is actually a word for an underwater earthquake. These particular waves were not being caused just by wind, but they were actually the result of a fissure under the lake splitting and causing a mini-tsunami! The King James Version of the Bible says the tempest was *"in the sea"* and not *"on the sea."* Jesus stood and rebuked the storm (v. 26), so if this storm was from God, then Christ was rebuking His heavenly Father when He rebuked the storm! This was a natural storm, and nothing spiritual was linked with it.

Based upon the whole of the Scriptures and examples too numerous to name, tsunami-type destruction, earthquakes, and even floods can come from one of three sources.

1.  God is the Creator of earth, wind, water, and fire, and base elements have been and will be used in the future to initiate judgments against the ungodly, including the future Great Tribulation.

2.  There are times when the disasters have nothing to do with God Himself initiating them, but are rather a reaction to the fact that the earth is old and has fault lines, cracks, and volcanic openings throughout its surface and underneath the seas. Blaming God for a normal natural disaster would be like a woman blaming her husband for the wrinkles appearing on her face. Some things are just a process of life. Since the whole of Creation is in travail, similar to a women who travails in labor prior to giving birth (Isa. 13:8; 21:3; Rom. 8:22), there will be seasons in which the cosmic heavens, the ground, and the seas will shake

and heave in travail, waiting for the day of the Messiah to bring deliverance to the planet (v. 22).

3. The evil in and around the earth, with the shedding of blood, causes the earth itself to disclose the blood of the slain, as the blood of the innocents cries out to God.

The death of innocent children is heartbreaking, tragic, and at times unexplainable. However, consider the nations in which the tsunami struck years ago. The fact is that in many of these nations the children do not enjoy the type of life and family relations that we in the West encounter. In many of these third-world nations both girls and boys are sold as sex slaves to sex-addicted adults who abuse and use them for their own perverted pleasure. God in His mercy may have allowed these children to be taken from the earth, and these innocent ones are with the Lord, safe from the hands of perverts, pedophiles, and sex trade organizations.

Another area where men and women struggle with their faith and a crack is found in their faith armor is when they see images of starving children in places such as Haiti and Africa. We have all been moved with tears of compassion when seeing the bloated stomachs of children, surrounded by starving siblings, sitting in the dust in a third-world nation, simply waiting for death. I have heard many believers say, "How can God allow this?"

I have visited and conducted evangelistic meetings in three African nations: Uganda, Kenya, and Zambia. In these and most nations in Africa there is a massive population of poor and starving people, many of whom are children, who cannot afford a loaf of bread and will possibly die at an early age. What most in the West are unaware of are the three main elements that, when mixed together, cause such poverty and lack.

1. The first element is the fact that many of the poor nations on earth are also nations dominated with the spirit of idolatry. The superstition of the people and ancient customs of their fathers cause them to turn to gods of wood and stone that are unable to hear one word uttered from their lips. Their prayers to their man-made gods go unheard, and their struggle never changes.

2. The second fact is that for many of these nations throughout modern history, millions of dollars in cash and food have been sent to the governments of these lands to distribute among their suffering population. In most instances these nations are under the control of one rich family or a dictator-type leader who places the money in his personal bank account in Switzerland and seizes the food shipments for himself and his military services, while the common people receive nothing. The true almighty God is not to be blamed for the lack of answered prayers addressed to idols or the actions of an ungodly dictator.

3. In numerous other nations food shortages are common as the weather patterns in these nations seem stuck in one mode—drought. Without rain and without the knowledge of planning and reaping, the uneducated masses thus sit with empty bellies and must depend upon the compassion of Christians and ministries worldwide to provide the provisions for survival.

For those who tend to continually blame God for the earth's trouble and distress, remember there is an evil agent the Bible calls the "god of this world" (2 Cor. 4:4, KJV) and the "prince of the power of the air" (Eph. 2:2), who blinds the understanding of men and thrives on the evil inclination within the dark part of the human heart.

## DAVID'S REACTION TO BAD NEWS

David miserably failed as a husband and friend when he impregnated the wife of Uriah, one of his choice mighty men. After sending the husband to the front line of a battle where he was slain, David married the woman, attempting to cover up his adulterous affair. Eventually the prophet Nathan pronounced a death sentence upon the household of David, calling it the "sword" (of the Lord, 2 Sam. 12:10). The infant who was conceived during the affair was born but was sickly from birth. David spent seven days fasting on his face in the dust in intercession before God, hoping God would reverse the decision and bring life to the infant. At the conclusion of the week David was informed the child had died. What would his reaction be after spending about 168 hours alone with God, with only one petition on his mind day and night— "God, heal my son."

Instead of blaming God, cursing Him for not being just and good, and questioning how God could take an infant when it was the sin of its father and not the sin of the child that angered the Lord, David's reaction surprised his closest friends. He arose from the dust, washed himself, and "went into the house of the LORD and worshiped" (v. 20). When asked why his reaction was such, the king answered:

> While the child was yet alive, I fasted and wept; for I said, "Who can tell whether the LORD will be gracious to me, that the child may live?" But now he is dead; why should I fast? Can I bring him back again? I shall go to him, but he shall not return to me.
>
> —2 SAMUEL 12:22–23

David understood that the soul and spirit of a human was eternal, and death was not the conclusion of life but an exit door for the soul, enabling the spirit to depart the fleshly shell and fly to the realm of eternal bliss. Thus the innocent infant's spirit was taken to the paradise of the Lord where David would eventually meet the spirit of the child when he passed.

When one of my dear minister friends lost one of his teenage children though a tragic accident, a well-known minister called to comfort him and his family. The caller had himself lost a daughter and son-in-law in a plane crash, and also his oldest son through a tragic death. In the midst of the darkest moments of this man's life, the Holy Spirit spoke to him and said, "There are things about this accident you will never know until you get to heaven." The Lord also instructed him not to question why it occurred; if he began to question, he would be questioning the rest of his life.

Our lives at times will experience a sudden and unexpected turn of events for which there is no simple explanation. As believers, our trust must always be in the Lord and in His sovereign decision-making process, as there will be things connected to the tragedy of which we are unaware and have no knowledge. Just determine in your heart that no matter what happens, you refuse to go to hell over a mystery.

# Chapter 11

# GETTING BACK YOUR MIND WHEN YOU'RE AT WITS' END

F OR A PERSON TO BE AT "WITS' END," HE OR SHE HAS COME to the end of the resources or strategies of how to solve a problem or deal with a person. Psalm 107:27–29 describes such an experience with these words:

> They reel to and fro, and stagger like a drunken man,
> And are at their wits' end.
> Then they cry out to the LORD in their trouble,
> And He brings them out of their distresses.
> He calms the storm,
> So that its waves are still.

The English word *wits'* here is interesting in the original Hebrew, as the Hebrew word is *chokmah* and refers to wisdom in a good sense. The commentary in the margin of one source reads: "All their wisdom is swallowed up."[1] The text is stating that a person has tried to be wise in their decision, and still trouble came and there was no way of escape. At times we do all we can do to resolve issues, only to say, "There is nothing left—now what?"

Coming to your wits' end is often the result of multiple attacks or combined challenges striking your job, family, health or finances at one time. I have often heard the expression, "Trouble comes in threes." This was true with Job when he lost his ten children, all of his livestock, and his health—three losses at one time. (See Job 1–2.) After Job's initial losses three "friends" arrived, attempting to explain the spiritual reason for his losses—although God later said that their opinions were not correct (Job 42:7). Three times trouble increases stress, for "a threefold chord is not quickly broken" (Eccles. 4:12). A threefold thread of difficulty can be woven to forge a stronghold, as indicated in the time King Saul ruled Israel:

> David therefore departed from there and escaped to the cave of Adullam. So when his brothers and all his father's house heard it, they went down there to him. And everyone who was in distress, everyone who was in debt, and everyone who was discontented gathered to him. So he became captain over them. And there were about four hundred men with him.
>
> —1 SAMUEL 22:1–2

This threefold chord was the "three Ds" of *distress, discontent,* and *debt.* King Saul had increased taxes on the people of Israel, and thus they were indebted, just as the national debt of America is causing every American to owe a debt to the Federal government that increases each week. The distress was a mental emotion as the people had no control over their circumstances or the national events occurring around them. Distress and debt lead to discontent, causing a lack of joy and peace and a restlessness that settles like a blanket over the people. These three sources of discouragement were enough to set people at their wits' end. Even David flirted with disaster at a place called Ziklag.

## The Ziklag Effect

In the setting of the narrative Saul had assigned his personal army to capture David at all cost. A report came that David had visited the high priest at a place called Nob. Saul interrogated the priests and discovered they had fed David the showbread from the golden table in the tabernacle. Saul was enraged and instructed eighty-five priests to be slaughtered (1 Sam. 22:19). As this word reached David, he also learned that his old friend, the prophet Samuel, had suddenly died (1 Sam. 25:1). As long as Samuel lived, David had a prayer covering. Now his head intercessor was gone. The third problem (remember trouble comes in threes) was Saul, who had discovered David's hiding place in the heart of the Judean wilderness (1 Sam. 26).

Thus all forms of David's protection and provision were now cut off. In the time of trouble David could go before the priest and inquire of the Lord at the tabernacle, to confirm or reconfirm his actions were or were not in God's will. Now the priests were dead. At times David would head to Ramah where Samuel and the sons of the prophets were headquartered. There he would be fed, encouraged, and hang out with men of like precious faith. Now this blessing was removed by the death of Samuel. In losing the priests David lost his *confirmation,* in losing Samuel he lost his *comfort,* and in losing the secrecy of his hiding place he now lost his *security.* David was at wits' end. Therefore he made a very strange decision. He left the land of Judah, his home tribe, and traveled south to the land of his enemies, the Philistines. He reasoned:

> And David said in his heart, "Now I shall perish someday by the hand of Saul. There is nothing better for me than that I should speedily escape to the land of the Philistines; and Saul will despair of me, to seek me anymore in any part of Israel. So I shall escape out of his hand."
>
> —1 Samuel 27:1

Why would David head toward the very people he had been fighting since a teenager? The answer is that David knew Saul was afraid of the Philistines and would not attack them in their own territory. When David went to fight the Philistine giant Goliath, the battle had been stuck for forty days, and Saul wasn't leading the charge to attack (1 Sam. 17). This is because the Spirit of the Lord was departing from him, and he had no confidence in his own natural ability.

There is another side to the story, however. If Saul had no *confidence* in himself, David was losing his *confidence* in God's promise for him to be king. Samuel anointed David, and God said he would be the next in line as king after Saul. But in 1 Samuel 27:1 David confessed that he should soon "perish one day by the hand of Saul." He chose the road of least resistance. The Philistines hated Saul, and Saul feared the Philistines, *so the enemy of my enemy is now my friend*.

The loss of a person's faith is a serious spiritual issue. In the parable of the unjust judge Christ asked, "When the Son of Man comes, will He really find faith on the earth?" (Luke 18:8). Even throughout the Torah God warned His chosen people not to forget His law and His benefits.

When David was confronted by the Philistine king, David said he was willing to fight against his own people, including Saul and his men. David had a large entourage of solders—six hundred—who were mighty men of war who followed him into battle. They were given a town called Ziklag as their headquarters, a place to move their wives and children. David's willingness to *fight against his own people* reminds me of how *wounded Christians are often willing to betray other believers*, exposing past secrets they know about others and verbally turning against their own church because of hurts and wounds. Ziklag was a town on the border of Judah. The idea in David's mind may have been that if Saul was after him, he could simply return to Ziklag, and if the Philistines turned on him, he could hop the fence and be back in Israel on Judah's side. However, the man who walks the middle of the road will eventually get hit from either direction!

## He Got Burnt

After returning from a battle, David discovered that Ziklag had been invaded by the Amalekites, who burned all the houses, took the valuables (spoil) the families owned, captured the wives and children of David and his men, and then fled the scene of their war crimes. As David and his men rode toward the city, a sickening feeling hit the pit of their stomachs when they saw columns of dark smoke and smelled the burning wood. When they arrived to the city, the popping sound of hot embers was replaced by the wails of grown men who had lost everything. Someone was to blame, and all fingers pointed to David. The distressed men made a decision to stone David. This would have been foolish, because stoning David would not bring back their wives and children. Instead of adding to the problem, they should be seeking a solution.

This is a real wits' end situation.

After losing the priests, Samuel, the hiding place—now everything is gone! David remembered that Abiathar had the ephod, a garment with stones that the priests used to inquire of the Lord (1 Sam. 30:7). After hitting bottom, David began looking up and sought the Lord for His will. God said, "Pursue, for you shall surely overtake them and without fail recover all" (v. 8). We read that David "encouraged himself in the LORD his God" (v. 6, KJV).

The three simple steps David followed at Ziklag are a practical application for believers today.

## 1. DAVID TURNED HIS CRISIS OVER TO THE LORD.

To whom would David turn for a sudden rescue from this mass death threat? The priests and Samuel were dead, his family was in Judah, and he was a stranger in the Philistines' stronghold, with six hundred of his closest associates planning on killing him. When David had nowhere else to turn to, he turned his face toward God. At times you may think you are waiting on heaven to move, but in reality, *heaven is waiting on earth!*

## 2. DAVID KNEW GOD WAS NOT FINISHED WITH HIM YET.

If David had really wanted to die and had lost all hope of his future, he would have yelled out, "Someone throw the first rock!" By consulting God, David knew the Lord wasn't finished with him yet. It is impossible to threaten to kill a man who has a divine assignment! Jonah came up from the bottom of the sea in the first "submarine ride" in a whale's belly and was preserved supernaturally because God had an assignment for Jonah yet to fulfill. Paul was stoned in Lystra, yet he arose after the disciples prayed and departed for his next mission trip because God had more places for Paul to minister (Acts 14). Even when he was bitten by a deadly viper and should have perished in minutes, the snake bite was harmless, as Paul's assignment was to win the island where he was shipwrecked to Christ. (See Acts 28.) You must believe that God has a plan and He is not finished with you yet!

## 3. DAVID ENCOURAGED HIMSELF IN THE LORD HIS GOD.

Notice David did not encourage himself in his warring ability, his wisdom, or his strength but in the "LORD his God" (1 Sam. 30:6, KJV). The root word in *encourage* is *courage*. If David were to pursue his enemies and overtake them, it would require a supernatural courage that only comes from God. This is the same boldness he sensed when as a teenager he stood before Goliath. (See 1 Samuel 17.)

## THE SICK EGYPTIAN

A part of the story that is often overlooked is the sick Egyptian.

> Then they found an Egyptian in the field, and brought him to David; and they gave him bread and he ate, and they let him drink water. And they gave him a piece of a cake of figs and two clusters of raisins. So when he had eaten, his strength came back to him; for he had eaten no bread nor drunk water for three days and three nights.
>
> —1 SAMUEL 30:11–12

David's enemies had a three-day head start and could have departed in any direction. However, David discovered a sick Egyptian in a field outside of Ziklag. He was a servant of one of the military commanders who had invaded Ziklag. Under an oath of protection from David, he "spilled the beans" and revealed the battle plan and the location where David's enemies had taken all the families and the possessions from the city. Imagine this. While the invasion is on, this Egyptian becomes deathly sick, and to avoid the sickness from spreading to the camp of the Amalekite army, the Amalekites dump the sick boy in a field!

All the time that David was out of God's will linking up with Israel's enemies, and during the moments that Ziklag was being burned and the wives and kids captured, the Lord is allowing one Egyptian servant, owned by the invaders, to become so sick that he gets thrown by the wayside. God was actually setting up David for a victorious outcome—three days before David ever knew that Ziklag was under attack! The provision for deliverance reminds me of when Abraham was walking Isaac up *one side* of Mount Moriah, preparing to lay him as a sacrifice on the altar, and a ram was walking up the *other side*, catching its horns in thick bushes, becoming the replacement for Isaac on the altar. (See Genesis 22.) In another narrative Christ knew taxes were due, and He needed additional income. He told Peter to go fishing and he would find a piece of money (coin) in a fish's mouth to pay His and Peter's taxes (Matt. 17:27). Before the tax was even due, a lone fish saw a shiny object, thinking it was a minnow, and while swallowing its "meal," it instead swallowed money.

At times you may believe that you are at wits' end and feel that God has bypassed you for a more urgent petition or a needier person. Perhaps He has "too many children" to take care of and is "too busy for you."

However, just as the examples above indicate, God prepares a good outcome before the situation arises; He is not surprised at the trouble and at your reaction to it, and He can and is planning a way of escape before you ever get into the crisis. Throughout the Book of Acts God warned Paul about specific trouble that would come his way, even leading to his arrest, but He also told him He would be with him and that Paul would one day stand before Caesar to testify.

Paul was arrested and, as a Roman citizen, had the legal right to appeal his case to the highest ruler of the Roman Empire, Caesar himself. Thus, during a public testimony, Paul said, "I appeal to Caesar" (Acts 25:11). Up until this moment Luke, the writer of Acts, records the negative and often life-threatening situations Paul faced, many times at the hands of religious Jews who saw this former Pharisee as a traitor and one who was corrupting the original intent of the Law of Moses by ministering to Gentiles. Paul's appeal to Caesar did two things.

First, it removed him from many of the cities where his persecutors were lying in wait to have him assaulted or arrested, taking him to Rome where Roman citizens had the full protection of the law on their side. Second, Paul was give two years of total freedom in his own hired house, ministering to all who came to him, no one hindering him (Acts 28:30–31). The Lord used the negative circumstances, including the persecution, to bring Paul to a point where he would appeal to Caesar, which gave him the opportunity to fulfill God's plan to preach the gospel to one of the most wicked Caesars in Roman history, Nero. Paul's work among the Roman believers was not in vain, as there was church in Caesar's house (Phil. 4:22).

The lives of David and Paul should encourage believers, as these two men present evidence that despite the numerous battles, struggles, and discouragements, God always works behind the scenes for your way of escape (1 Cor. 10:13) or to lead you into a deeper part of His will. *There is always a Ziklag battle before a Zion victory.*

*Chapter 12*

# WHEN a *SKANDALON* CRACKS YOUR SHIELD

XXXX

WHEN AN ENGAGED MAN CALLS OFF HIS WEDDING, IT IS A common expression for someone to say, "He broke her heart." The heart is a flesh and blood organ that pumps blood throughout the body; thus, how can a fleshly organ be *broken*? Research is now discovering that the actual physical heart is much more than a blood pump.[1] The Lord had much to say about the heart. The human mind has the ability to see images and process information. Both the heart and the brain have a specific life force. In the brain the life force is the soul, and in the heart there is a conscience linked to the soul.

The brain is the three-pound physical computer that runs the entire body. Part of the brain function contains the mind, which I consider the hard drive of the brain, linking it to the five senses: hearing, seeing, smelling, tasting, and touching, from which we derive all information and knowledge of the physical world. The soul is the supernatural life force that gives life, linking thoughts to the body, and is also the part of the mind that senses and discerns spiritual truths and spiritual knowledge. It is odd how a human using his or her mind can accept or learn truth and error, unrighteousness and righteousness, faith and unbelief, peace and confusion, and basically become a well of knowledge or a field for battle.

Prophetic teachers often point to the Olivet Discourse to glean insight concerning signs and events to unfold at the time of the end. Often ministers mention wars, rumors of wars, famine, pestilences, earthquakes, and other negative signs (Matt. 24:4–7), but they omit one of the most significant personal signs that all believers must be warned of, and that is the sign of offense.

In prophetic conferences I have heard detailed statistics on the increased number of earthquakes, plagues, and diseases, along with the increase in civil and national wars. At times the speaker concludes with Matthew 24:13: "But he who endures to the end shall be saved." The speaker implies that "enduring to the end" refers to enduring the many disasters, diseases, and possibilities of death lurking in these global calamities. It would be like saying, "It is going to get rough out there, and if you can survive and endure these signs, you will be saved in the end."

However, if you will study Matthew 24:13 in the context of what was previously said, there is a different light of understanding that comes forth.

> Then they will deliver you up to tribulation and kill you, and you will be hated by all nations for My name's sake. And then many will be offended, will betray one another, and will hate one another. Then many false prophets will rise up and deceive many. And because lawlessness will abound, the love of many will grow cold. But he who endures to the end shall be saved.
>
> —MATTHEW 24:9–13

What Christ is revealing is that at the time of the end men and women will be so sensitive to offense that many will not be able to endure offenses and will retaliate by betraying and hating their offenders and speaking evil about them.

What does Christ refer to when instructing to "endure until the end"? The end of what? The English word *end* is found five times just in Matthew 24 and has three different applications.

1. Christ uses the word in verse 3 concerning signs of His coming and the "end of the age." This word *end* refers to the consummation and completion of the age of man's government and control on earth.

2. In verse 6 Christ then refers to wars and rumors of wars as a sign of His coming but informs His audience that "the end is not yet." The end here alludes to the conclusion or the uttermost point of something.

3. When we arrive at verse 13—"endures to the end"— the word *end* here refers to the conclusion.

Back to the question of *enduring to the end of what?* There are three possibilities Christ is referring to according to three different interpretations given by scholars. The first is enduring till the end of the destruction of Jerusalem—which occurred in AD 70. History recounts that the community of Christians living in Jerusalem immediately prior to 70 evacuated Jerusalem when the attack began and settled in Pella in Jordan, as prophesied in Matthew 24:15–16. They built a thriving community there while Jerusalem burned to the ground. Thus they endured until the end of the destruction of the city.

The second interpretation by some is that if you, as a believer, can remain faithful through the bad things occurring during your lifetime, then you can make it till the end and be saved—or enter the eternal kingdom of God by enduring the persecutions and pressures of life, thus having lived an overcoming life.

The third interpretation, as stated above, is surviving the negative circumstances sweeping the earth prior to the return of Christ. Many will fall, suffer, and give up, but others will endure until the "end."

There is, however, a fourth possibility that is more plausible in light of the context of Christ's statement. Christ was warning that "many will be offended" (v. 10). The Greek word for "offense" is *skandalon,* which originally referred to the bait on a trap that attracts the animal. The root word means, "to jump up, snap shut," and the *skandalethron* was the arm of the stick where the bait was set. We derive our English words *scandal* and *scandalize* from this word. When a trap is set for an animal, there must be some form of camouflage to hide it from the sight of the unsuspecting creature. However, the smell of the bait, like a magnet to a magnet, pulls the animal off its journey to investigate the bait, and suddenly the trap catches the animal.

By Christ's time the word referred to any stumbling block put in a man's way that would trip him up and cause him to fall.[2] The strategy behind an offense is to cause a person to stumble, fall, or participate in certain behavior that will cause ruin or destruction.

This word is used is a variety of examples throughout the New Testament. The word was used by Greek writers (such as Aristophanes) for the "verbal traps" set to lure a person into an argument in order to trip them up.[3] In Matthew 13:21, in the parable of the sower, there are some who are offended at the instruction required by God's Word, and thus they turn from Christ because of persecution. The spiritual design of persecution is to use verbal assaults, like burning arrows, to insult a person and place mental pressure upon a believer, causing that person to choose serving Christ with persecutions or departing the faith for convenience. The apostate who departs has fallen to the offense, or the *skandalon*, as the *bait of persecution* created internal and emotional pressure that he or she could not stand up under. When the Pharisees attempted to trap Christ with controversial questions, Paul wrote that the preaching of the cross and crucifixion of Christ was a "stumbling block" to the Jews of his day (Rom. 14:13; 1 Cor. 1:23; Gal. 5:11). This was because in the Torah, the Law said that any man who was hung on a tree was cursed (Deut. 21:22–23).

Enduring to the end, in the context, has nothing to do with surviving a plague, crawling out alive from the rubble of an earthquake, or hiding in a mountain until a war ceases. It refers to a person who can endure the many offenses and verbally set traps that will be encountered until the time of the return of Christ. If you were to do a survey in the average church, and reach out to those who once attended but are no longer in the pews, you will discover (as I have) that a majority of former church attendees were offended by the pastor or a church staffer or a fellow member, and now they sit at home refusing to attend any church at all. They now perceive that all Christians and ministers are *hypocrites!* I cannot tell you the number of individuals I have personally encountered during more than thirty-five years of ministry who stay at home on Sunday while their family attends church because they engaged in a verbal conflict, a difference of opinion, or heard a particular message from the pulpit that offended them in some manner. No amount of invitations and baiting them can bring them into a church as long as they are entrapped in the offense. Solomon said it this way: "A brother offended is harder to win than a strong city, and contentions are like the bars of a castle" (Prov. 18:19).

How do we endure? The word *endure* comes from two words: *hupo*, meaning "under," and *phero*, meaning "to bear." The imagery of the original Greek word was that of a plant that had been trampled on yet continued to rise again and again. It means to have the strength to bear pressure without collapsing or being destroyed by the weight. Paul understood this when he spoke of having a hindering spirit that buffeted him (2 Cor. 12:7), meaning that this spirit was continually harassing him and causing him difficulty. He would be hit, then stand up only to be hit again. Paul said in 2 Corinthians 4:8–9: "We are hard pressed on every side, yet not crushed; we are perplexed, but not in despair; persecuted, but not forsaken; struck down, but not destroyed." Paul learned that "in whatever state I am, to be content: I know how to be abased, and I know how to abound. Everywhere and in all things I have learned both to be full and to be hungry, both to abound and to suffer need" (Phil. 4:11–12). The key was in this fact: "I can do all things through Christ who strengthens me" (v. 13).

## THE MINISTRY OF A "PROPHA-LIAR"

If you are still breathing on this planet, you will at some point be stabbed in the back, be evil spoken of, and have the opportunity to be offended. Different people react differently to offenses. When reading the context of the warning of offense, I observed that just one verse after Christ warned of many being offended, He warned that "many false prophets will rise up and deceive many" (Matt. 24:11). Oddly, He repeats the same warning in verse 24, referring to "false christs and false prophets." What warning is linked to being offended and false prophets?

Let me illustrate something I have personally seen as a pastor's son growing up in a full gospel church. Most full gospel people believe the Lord can and does at times speak to His people through the Holy Spirit and through the vocal gifts (1 Cor. 12:7–10). The blessing of this manifestation is that a believer can receive confirmation of God's will through these gifts, while the negative is that a carnal person may attempt to manipulate others by operating in what appears to be a vocal gift but is a verbal statement from their own spirit. This happened in Jeremiah's time, when we read:

> And the LORD said to me, "The prophets prophesy lies in My name. I have not sent them, commanded them, nor spoken to them; they prophesy to you a false vision, divination, a worthless thing, and the deceit of their heart."
>
> —JEREMIAH 14:14

Jeremiah was warning of the coming Babylonian destruction of Jerusalem, while the false prophets at the temple were saying that prosperity was coming and the enemy would be defeated. These were two opposite predictions, and the people were confused as to who was truly speaking on God's behalf. Of course, when the destruction arrived, Jeremiah's name was made known as the true seer of the Almighty.

When an individual in a church becomes offended, they may attempt to pull others into their offense.

At the peak of their offense some seek out a *confirmation* that their negative attitude against the pastor or leadership is "approved" by the Lord. There is always at least one self-acclaimed and self-anointed prophet or prophetess in the church who will come to the aid of the offended soul and begin to prophesy that "God told me to tell you to leave this church because the glory of God has departed from it," or, "They have offended us and need to be exposed." An offended person will either react in the manner of Korah or of David.

Korah was a noted, wealthy prince of Israel who led a rebellion with 250 other leaders against Moses and Aaron, which eventually cost him his life and the lives of all the rebels with him (Num. 16). David was being hunted like a wild beast by his angry and jealous father-in-law, King Saul, and had opportunity to kill Saul twice. However, David refused to do evil against Saul, as David understood the spiritual authority God had given Saul (1 Sam. 26:5–11). It is easy for offended persons to seek out a false prophetic word that pours a little oil on the wound and makes them feel better about accepting their offense as a useful weapon to defeat the opposing side. Offended people are not afraid to betray and hate their offender, thus causing their love to wax cold and their conscience to become seared and calloused.

## DID JOHN THE BAPTIST GET OFFENDED?

John the Baptist was a cousin to Jesus, as Christ's mother, Mary, and John's mother, Elizabeth, were also cousins. John was born six months prior to Christ; both were about thirty years of age when John was baptizing believers in the Jordan River and Christ came to the Jordan to be baptized of John (Luke 3:23). John introduced Christ as the "Lamb of God" and informed his own followers that he must decrease and Christ must increase (John 1:29; 3:30).

Shortly after Christ's baptism Herod had John arrested and imprisoned for his politically incorrect statements made against Herod's illegal marriage. While John was in prison, several of his disciples visited him. John sent them back to ask Christ a very interesting and rather odd question. John said to ask: "Are You the Coming One [the Messiah], or do we look for another?" (Matt. 11:3). Was John confused about Christ? He previously introduced Christ as the Lamb of God, and he knew he was to prepare the way (Matt. 3:3) and then to step out of the way. John was the first to announce that Christ would baptize believers with the Holy Ghost and fire (v. 11, KJV). When John's disciples asked if Christ was the One (the expected Messiah), Christ's answered John with these words:

> Go and tell John the things which you hear and see: The blind see and the lame walk; the lepers are cleansed and the deaf hear; the dead are raised up and the poor have the gospel

preached to them. And blessed is he who is not offended
because of Me.

—MATTHEW 11:4–6

Christ revealed that the miracles being performed were the sign
Christ was the Messiah. But why did Christ conclude His answer
by telling John he is blessed if he is not offended in Christ? This
is perplexing until one understands the possible *coded message* John
was sending Christ. If Christ was the Messiah, then He had both
supernatural power and political influence to get John released from
this prison cell. Christ's answer indicated that He had no intention
of releasing John and that He wanted John not to open the door
of his heart to an offense. Christ was not going to do what John
wanted done—initiate a prison break. Christ knew that the Law
and prophets were to be obeyed until the time of John, and Christ
was now on the scene to announce that the kingdom of heaven
was at hand (Matt. 4:17). If Christ was not the awaited Messiah
and another was coming in the future, it would indicate that John
could enjoy more ministry time to people in the future and would
not die in prison. Christ did not release His cousin, and shortly
after this, John was beheaded by Herod (Matt. 14:10). *Christ knew
John's future, but John was uncertain of his future.* Christ wanted John
to avoid offense when things did not go the way John hoped.

## OFFENDED AT GOD

Throughout my ministry I have encountered men and women who
were very angry at God for not answering a prayer in the manner
they prayed or expected. I have actually observed some believers
who lived their lives in a careless fashion, sowing their wilds oats,
only to produce an unexpected wild harvest of trouble, for which
these people then blamed God for not causing a drought and preventing the bad seed they planted early from sprouting later in their
garden of life.

One woman was having difficulty in her marriage and met a man on a trip. She began calling him on the phone and eventually had consensual sex one night. It was *intended* to be a one-night stand with no harm done to anyone.

However, she became pregnant, and the man threatened to sue her for the custody of the child. The woman was overwhelmed and angry that the Lord did not somehow prevent her from becoming pregnant with another man's child. Blaming God for this conception would be like a lifetime smoker becoming angry at the Almighty for not preventing him from getting cancer after consuming thousands of packs of cigarettes. It would be like playing Russian roulette and cursing God because when you pulled the trigger, the single bullet struck you and not the others. God protects the righteous from danger, but there is no provision of protection for the disobedient. Just ask Jonah.

All humans are subject to human circumstances. The earth is in travail and responds with storms, earthquakes, hurricanes, and tornados that rip apart entire communities, at times taking the lives of innocent men, women, and children. The fleshly body begins to show age, and our bones began to creak like the boards in an old house, while our pace of life goes from the speed of a race car to a Model T. Age brings the death of friends and loved ones, various forms of affliction in the body, and new cares of life that we must learn to cast on the Lord (1 Pet. 5:7). Paul understood this truth and wrote a wonderful and encouraging passage reminding believers to hold on, because trials will not last forever:

> And since we have the same spirit of faith, according to what is written, "I believed and therefore I spoke," we also believe and therefore speak, knowing that He who raised up the Lord Jesus will also raise us up with Jesus, and will present us with you. For all things are for your sakes, that grace, having spread through the many, may cause thanksgiving to abound

to the glory of God. Therefore we do not lose heart. Even though our outward man is perishing, yet the inward man is being renewed day by day. For our light affliction, which is but for a moment, is working for us a far more exceeding and eternal weight of glory.

—2 Corinthians 4:13–17

Paul was beaten three times with rods, five times with forty stripes save one, three times he was shipwrecked, arrested on numerous occasions (2 Cor. 11:23–27), and he calls this persecution "our light affliction"! He did so understanding that our trials and tribulations only last for a "moment."

Perhaps Psalm 119:165 sums up the attitude believers should take toward offense: "Great peace have those who love Your law, and nothing causes them to stumble"—nothing will trip them up and cause them to fall. As you spiritually mature and the lines of time form tiny marks on your face, you will awake to the realization that you now have a limited time on earth. Perhaps then you will realize that life is too short to spend chained in the cave of unforgiveness, hiding from the faces of friends and family for the sake of protecting old wounds.

There is one type of person who is totally impossible to offend—and I mean that nothing you do or say can get that person to respond in a negative manner—and that is *a dead man*. If you attend his homegoing service at the local funeral home, you could comment to others (please don't, however), "That is the ugliest-looking suit I have ever seen on him," or "That makeup on his face looks like someone out of a horror movie," or "Man, don't he look like he's aged twenty years!" Say what you wish, but you cannot and will not offend him—because he can't hear you.

Paul said, "I die daily" (1 Cor. 15:31). If you are the type of person who must always be bragged on, told how good you are, and need a consistent, daily pat on the back, you will be in serious trouble throughout your life as—I hate to tell you—some people are not going to like you. In my own ministry, when I preach on prophecy, some disagree with my interpretation, or when I minister on the Holy Spirit, some reject the teaching. There are people who for whatever reason do not appreciate the messages or methods I use in ministry. However, it is hard to offend a dead man. *I have chosen to become dead to the critics and simply do God's will the best I can.*

In my earlier ministry I would become offended at the negative comments, until I discovered the seed of offense was being birthed out of a bruised ego and a slight amount of pride. When you desire to be liked by people and are disliked by some, the human ego will mentally enlarge the few as though they are many, and soon you are swimming in a dirty pool of offenses. After years of dealing with trying to understand why some people disliked me or the ministry, I chose to just die out to their comments, as it is simply their opinion and all men have a right to their own opinion. Not everyone liked Jesus, Paul, or the members of the early church, so I am in good company. Never let the negative opinions of others pull you down to their level. Life it too short, eternity too long, and offense too dangerous to risk the disfavor of God by walking in the mud of offense and tracking it into your church, home, and family.

*Chapter 13*

# USING THE WRONG SWORD
# FOR THE WRONG BATTLE

THE BELIEVER HAS A MIGHTY WEAPON IN THE SWORD OF the Spirit, which is the Word of God (Eph. 6:17). The Word of God was written on parchments with black ink and quill pens and was later translated to numerous languages, being printed on paper using the printing presses. God's Word, however, is not just to be read but spoken, and not just spoken but believed and acted upon. The fact that the Word of God is called a "two-edged sword" is not just for creating the image of a Roman soldier's weapon, but also to emphasize the fact that the Word has two sharp edges. One edge was formed when the Word was revealed by the Holy Spirit to the prophets who wrote the Scripture on the parchments. The other side of the blade is forged when a believer begins to speak out of his or her mouth the words that are written on paper.

Just as a sharp two-edged sword must be properly handled by the owner, lest he unintentionally cut himself or harm others, the Word of God must be properly interpreted, clearly spoken, and taught with the same care as man flashing a sharp sword in a crowd of people.

## MISHANDLING THE SCRIPTURES

You would never ask an untrained solder to join a frontline battle, or a student driver to drive in a NASCAR race, or a ministry novice to present a theological discourse at a seminary. Yet men and women continually misquote, misuse, and abuse others by mishandling the Scriptures. Here are a few examples.

### USING SCRIPTURE OUT OF CONTEXT

When scriptures are taken out of their context, meaning out of the historical or contextual setting in which they were written, then a person can become confused and think the Bible is contradicting itself. For example, several years ago I saw a photograph that was taken in the Greenbush Cemetery near Lafayette, Indiana. Near the granite grave maker was the tombstone of a Christian soldier who had died in a war. The marker had the image of the Good Shepherd, Christ, on it and was facing toward the east, which is the direction of a traditional Christian burial, since Matthew 24:27 states that the coming of the Lord is as lightning coming from the east. Near this marker was an older marker with these words inscribed:

> Martin P. Jenners
> Was born August 21, 1832, in a log cabin on the Northwest
> Corner of Ferry and Fourth Streets
> Died December 22, 1919
> My only objection to religion is that is not true
> 1 Corinthians 15:52; Isaiah 26:14
> No preaching, no praying, no psalm reading permitted on
> this lot

Below are the two verses that were embedded in the granite marker that caused Mr. Jenners to believe that religion was not true:

> In a moment, in the twinkling of an eye, at the last trump: for the trumpet shall sound, and the dead shall be raised incorruptible, and we shall be changed.
>
> —1 CORINTHIANS 15:52, KJV

> They are dead, they will not live; they are deceased, they shall not rise: therefore thou hast visited and destroyed them, and made all their memory to perish.
>
> —ISAIAH 26:14, KJV

It appears that this man fell for one of the oldest tricks in the adversary's playbook—that the Bible is full of contradictions and cannot be trusted. Mr. Jenners read each verse by itself, without ever following one of the first laws of biblical interpretation, which is, "What is the context of what is being spoken, and to whom was it spoken?"

The entire chapter of 1 Corinthians 15 is where Paul is revealing the mystery of the resurrection of the dead and how in the "twinkling of an eye" the dead in Christ will be raised. Isaiah 26:14 appears to contradict this promise, as it says they are dead and will not rise. However, in the context of this chapter the prophet was dealing with nations that had risen up against Israel and were no longer in existence—yet Israel still endured. This death had no reference to individual people but to empires and nations in the past that mistreated the Jews and no longer existed. Thus one verse deals with the bodily resurrection of the dead in Christ and the other with nations who ceased to exist and had no chance of being raised again in the future.

Satan actually attempted this "bait and switch" strategy during the temptation of Christ (Matt. 4:5–6) when he suggested that

Christ could throw Himself from the top of the pinnacle of the temple and would never be harmed, because if He were God's Son, then God would gladly provide angels to scoop down to prevent His premature death. Satan based his suggestion (temptation) on Psalm 91:11–12 (KJV):

> For he shall give his angels charge over thee, to keep thee in all thy ways. They shall bear thee up in their hands, lest thou dash thy foot against a stone.

In Matthew 4:6 (KJV) the phrase, "lest at any time" was added to this passage, not by the translators but by Satan himself when quoting the passage—suggesting that if Jesus ever felt like jumping from a high place, the angels would always be there. This was taking the passage *out of context*, as the verses before this in Psalm 91 deal with God protecting His people from evil; it has nothing to do with willfully falling from a high place or jumping from a mountain to prove some point to a skeptic. Guard against someone taking the Word of God out of the context that was intended.

## Using Scripture for personal gain

One of the great dangers in our generation is unscrupulous ministers who have been successful at using what I call the "prosperity lottery" for personal gain. The message is that is if you will read it right, believe it right, speak it right, think it right, and "send me a check with your largest offering," then your name is entered by the Lord Himself into His special "prosperity lottery," where God will eventually call your name out for free money, a new house and a new car, and you won't have to work for it or pay for it. These types of ministers are those whom Peter warned about: "By covetousness they will exploit you with deceptive words; for a long time their judgment has not been idle, and their destruction does not slumber" (2 Pet. 2:3).

I have heard some of the most unbiblical claims made and promises and blessings pronounced when ministers have been seeking money to expand their ministry. For your "best gift" you can be guaranteed to be debt free the rest of your life. Folks, the only way you will never have debt is if you never purchase anything again the rest of your life or if you die—then you have no debts to pay on earth. If you pay taxes each year, rent an apartment, and pay any insurance, then you have a debt. I have heard special anointing promised for a large seed offering. This is like Simon the sorcerer attempting to purchase the gift of the Holy Ghost from Peter, who after being offered money rebuked this Samaritan sorcerer and told him his heart was bitter and not right with God (Acts 8:18–23). Peter made it clear that the gift of God cannot be purchased with money (v. 20).

## USING THE "SWORD" ON FELLOW SOLDIERS

In the body of Christ there are occasionally disagreements in certain aspects of theology. It is interesting to see how one denomination takes a certain passage to prove their point, while another denomination *quotes the same reference* to disprove the argument of the other group! One of those issues is speaking with tongues. One group that teaches certain gifts have ceased quotes the latter half of 1 Corinthians 13 as a proof text that "tongues...will cease" (v. 8). According to some theologians, certain gifts have ceased either after the death of the original apostles or when the New Testament canon of Scripture was compiled to form our Bible. Another full gospel group will simply turn to 1 Corinthians 1:7, where Paul wrote, "So that you come short in no gift, eagerly waiting for the revelation of our Lord Jesus Christ," and Romans 11:29, "For the gifts and calling of God are irrevocable," to prove from these verses that the gift (Greek, *charismata*) of God, including the nine charismata (gifts) of the Holy Spirit (1 Cor. 12:7–10), are presently available until the coming of Christ!

It has always been disheartening to watch fellow believers turning the Bible into their own personal sword to attack other believers simply because they disagree with their doctrinal interpretations. Some are so adamant that they alone are correct that they tag anyone who disagrees with them as a *heretic*. Some ministers emphasize the teaching of the cross, which is of course the theme of Paul's ministry—to know nothing save the cross and Christ crucified (1 Cor. 2:2). *However, in all of Paul's preaching of the cross, not once did he ever use the cross in an attempt to crucify someone on it!* I have heard ministers proclaim the redemptive, cleansing power of the cross with one breath and minutes later begin calling names of very godly men and women of God, calling them "enemies of the cross" and trying to publicly humiliate these ministers, all in the name of defending the faith!

This is the same spirit that Christ's disciples had when He had sent several disciples to inform the Samaritans that this Jewish prophet, Jesus, wanted to pass through their territory. The Samaritans rejected the offer, and James and John informed Christ of the city's negative reaction and petitioned for Christ to send fire from heaven and burn the entire city to the ground. At that time Jews and Samaritans despised one another, as the Jews considered Samaritans an ethnically mixed group—part Jew and part Gentile. The angry disciples even used the Bible to justify their request to call fire down on them the way Elijah did against Baal's prophets on Mount Carmel (Luke 9:54). Jesus rebuked them, informing them they had the wrong spirit (v. 55). Many years later the evangelist Philip preached in Samaria, and the entire city received the gospel. Converts were baptized in the Holy Spirit, and other cities and towns were reached with the message of Christ (Acts 8:5–25). This attitude of "turn or burn" was not the right spirit from a group of men who had already been informed that Christ came to seek and to save that which was lost (Matt. 18:11).

Scripture must be used to preach the gospel, encourage the believer, convict the sinner, and correct error that may arise. However, it is wrong for ministers and denominations to get in a "sword fight," especially in public, as it only causes the sinners to mock and become more hardened as they watch two Christians duke it out to see who can knock the other one down "for the glory of God."

USING SCRIPTURE TO APPROVE OF YOUR DISOBEDIENCE

Another danger of using the sword of the Spirit in the wrong manner is when Scripture is interpreted in an attempt to justify, by certain verses, a person's disobedience. Several years ago I turned on a live feed from Washington DC where a group of pro-choice women were promoting abortion rights for women. I was stunned when a Jewish woman stood and said, "Even the Torah is on our side." I leaned forward in disbelief. What verse would she quote to prove that God is pro-choice? She then said: "God said for people to choose, over and over again in the Torah. So we are pro-choice because even God allows us to choose what we wish." I could imagine an ignorant American who believed in aborting an infant drooling with pleasure at that moment, not knowing that the woman misrepresented the Torah and used a verse out of context to approve of her actions. At that moment I jumped up and said, "Read what God said to choose:

> I call heaven and earth as witnesses today against you, that I
> have set before you life and death, blessing and cursing; there-
> fore choose life, that both you and your descendants may live.
> —DEUTERONOMY 30:19–20

Moses did write to "choose," but to "choose life"! When a woman chooses life and gives birth to her child, her descendants will live! This methodology of self-interpreting a scripture has been a method of abuse among carnal ministers and members. In our generation there have been ministers who have divorced their wife for another woman, as she was "a better choice for their ministry." They had no biblical basis, and when confronted, some quoted the verse that says that a bishop is to be the "husband of one wife" (1 Tim. 3:2, 12; Titus 1:6). One man's response was, "According to some scholars, this means one wife at a time!" I have also known men who left their wives for another woman and would use the story of David and Bathsheba, saying, "David committed adultery, and the Lord let him remain as the king, so I can continue in what I am doing because I am God's anointed too!" They seldom bring out the fact that the judgment of God came to David's house, and four of his sons (the infant from Bathsheba, Amnon, Absalom, and Adonijah) experienced a premature death as the sword never departed his house (2 Sam. 12:10).

## USING SCRIPTURE TO PULL IN YOUR OWN FOLLOWING

In my lifetime I have observed ministers who spend the majority of their radio or television airtime attempting to correct all of the errors they see in other ministries. I have heard an unwise novice call other believers by name and accuse them of false doctrine, false teaching, and heresy. When I personally would review the accused minister's teachings they were criticizing, I discovered the critic was simply pulling certain quotes out of context and making a major issue out of a minor disagreement. In some cases, the accusers have a huge beam in their own eye of past disobedience or sin in their life and are attempting to build a cultlike following through swishing a sword and cutting anyone in their path.

The reality is that these critics are appealing to a certain segment of the Christian community that I identify as "self-appointed watch dogs" or "heresy hunters" who literally thrive off of controversy as a politician does off of major endorsements. These lovers of criticism feed the overblown egos of these outspoken swashbucklers with words like: "You are the only one preaching the truth." "Tell it like it is." "Let them have it." "You are God's voice for the nation." The second observation is that if one man can convince his listeners that everyone else is wrong except him and his chosen few, then the financial support will only flow in the direction of this teacher.

Many years ago I recalled a minister announcing on his program that he was "the only one in the world called to take the gospel to the world, and the only minister who was doing it." I knew this was pride gone to roost as the body of Christ was much bigger than one man's television ministry, and the church—not just one man— was chosen and called to take the gospel to the world (Matt. 24:14). The sad and dangerous thing was that he really believed what he was saying! Anyone who boasts pridefully is slashing out and cutting down other believers who are also doing the same work of the kingdom, perhaps in a different manner. These prideful ministers need to know that they don't know what manner of spirit they are of (Luke 9:51–55).

## THE PROPER WAY TO USE THE SWORD OF THE SPIRIT

Paul wrote his last letter to Timothy and said:

> Preach the word! Be ready in season and out of season. Convince, rebuke, exhort, with all longsuffering and teaching.
> —2 TIMOTHY 4:2

We think of the word *preach* as a minister standing behind a pulpit giving a sermon or message to the congregation. Among the ancient Greeks this Greek word, *kerusso*, pictured the herald of the emperor standing before the masses in a city giving an important, even a life-and-death message to the people. The herald was the voice for the emperor and spoke with the same authority of the emperor. The minister is to "rebuke" when needed, meaning to rebuke sin in the lives of the people to bring them to repentance.

Paul warned Timothy of two men who were spiritually dangerous in the church: Hymenaeus and Philetus. These false teachers had taught the resurrection was past and had overthrown the faith of some weak believers in the church (2 Tim. 2:18). Paul said this false teaching corrupted the faith of some and "will eat as doth a canker" (v. 17, KJV). The Greek word for "canker" here is *gaggraina*, which alluded to an ulcer that gnaws on the skin or in the physical body. This is where we derive the English word *gangrene*—an infection that eats away at the tissue of the body and, if untreated, can eventually cause death. A severely diseased limb with gangrene must be amputated. Here, Paul is instructing the church to shun (separate from) Hymenaeus and Philetus as their teaching was corrupting and spreading throughout the church like gangrene!

This reveals the proper way to use the sword of the Spirit, in the sense of *cutting away false teaching* or exposing dangerous heretical doctrine, contrary to the revelation of the Scriptures. The Word of God has a piercing power and divides the soul and spirit, meaning the thoughts of man from the thoughts of God (Heb. 4:12). Christ, Paul, and all of the apostles wielded the Old Testament into a powerful weapon of war to defend the Christ as the Messiah, using the Torah and the Prophets, and building their doctrine on the words of Christ and revelation from God Himself (Gal. 1:12; 2:2). Let me point out, it is for the purpose of cutting away false doctrine and not cutting down to the ground someone who has a difference of opinion or a different method of ministry than you do.

Some of the false teaching spreading like gangrene in the body of Christ is:

- Hell does not exist.

- All men will end up in heaven no matter what religion they are (universalism).

- God approves of same-sex relations.

- Abortion is only a surgical procedure, as the fetus is not a human until the umbilical cord is cut.

- The Bible cannot be trusted, is outdated, and not relevant for the culture.

Instead of wasting their airtime rebuking Christian youth groups for being "of the devil" because of the "contemporary music," or viewing home Bible studies as "not of God," ministers should quit wasting time shadowboxing some invisible, imaginary enemy. Ministers should be taking the two-edged sword and forging another reformation—a return to the sound doctrine of the prophets and apostles of the Christian faith. Never use the message of the cross to crucify those you don't like, or the sword of the Spirit to attack other believers. The desire of Christ is revealed in this passage:

> And other sheep I have which are not of this fold; them also I must bring, and they will hear My voice; and there will be one flock and one shepherd.
>
> —JOHN 10:16

The body of Christ needs unity, not more division.

## BEWARE OF GIANTS WITH NEW SWORDS

The adversary is a master counterfeiter! Scripture is identified as "the sword of the Spirit" for its ability to divide the carnal from the spiritual (Heb. 4:12) and cut out the desire for sin and disobedience. The enemy, however, has his own arsenal of weapons to counter the weapons of God.

In King David's time there were five giants dwelling in Israel, with Goliath being the most noted (1 Sam. 17; 2 Sam. 21:15–21). After slaying Goliath, David took Goliath's sword, cut the giant's head off, and later took the sword as a spoil of his war victory

(1 Sam. 21:9). Many years later David fought a giant who had created a "new sword." We read:

> Then Ishbi-Benob, who was one of the sons of the giant, the weight of whose bronze spear was three hundred shekels, who was bearing a new sword, thought he could kill David.
>
> —2 SAMUEL 21:16

If you have gained a major spiritual victory over the world, flesh, or the devil, your adversary refuses to be idle and allow you to a long-term victory parade. He will return to his war room and design a *new sword* and wait for the appropriate time to challenge you in another battle. I cannot recount the times I have heard someone say, "I have never encountered a spiritual battle quite like this one!" This is because it is a new giant with a new sword.

Today the true church is engaged in a conflict with *new swords*, or numerous new doctrines that are emerging in a culture that prizes being *politically correct* over being *spiritually truthful*. These *new swords*, called "doctrines of demons," are being wielded through the influence of seducing spirits (1 Tim. 4:1, KJV). For example, some former evangelical ministers are teaching that all religions lead to heaven, as others are preaching that every human will eventually be in heaven no matter what they believed. Just as the new giant with the new sword almost killed David, these new teachings are set to destroy the truth and dull the true sword of God's Word. A totally dull knife, ax, or sword may look beautiful, but it is useless for what it was created for. Believers who water down the Word of God, weakening the strong taste of biblical doctrine, will find themselves anemic and weak from a lack of nourishment from God's heavenly manna.

Instead of using our biblical knowledge to assault other believers who may differ occasionally with us on minor issues, we should minimize and reduce the impact of the enemy's weapons by exploding the knowledge of the truth on the world scene, as the gospel must be preached around the world before the end will come (Matt. 24:14). Your enemy is not a Baptist, Pentecostal, or charismatic—your enemy is a destroyer of souls called Satan and his spirit rebels (Eph. 6:12). *You can't fight right unless you're in the light*—and the light is the Word of God.

## Chapter 14

# REVIVING THE ANCIENT BATTLE STRATEGIES FOR MODERN SPIRITUAL WAR

C HRIST MINISTERED IN ISRAEL AT A TIME WHEN ROMAN soldiers were occupying the land, and conflict would arise between the people and the government. The government always won the argument. It was Christ who said:

> Or what king, going to make war against another king, does not sit down first and consider whether he is able with ten thousand to meet him who comes against him with twenty thousand? Or else, while the other is still a great way off, he sends a delegation and asks conditions of peace.
>
> —LUKE 14:31–32

In these last days there will be a bombardment of assaults of strategic proportions designed against the believers. Paul warned of seducing spirits and doctrines of devils to be unleashed in the latter times (1 Tim. 4:1, KJV). Christ warned of spiritual deception and false prophets (Matt. 24:4, 11). There will also be widespread offenses that will cause friends to turn against one another (vv. 10–12). These spiritual struggles are combined with an atmosphere of great fear (Luke 21:26), great wrath (Rev. 12:12), and a future great tribulation (Matt. 24:21). Peter predicted that in the last days men would mock and scoff at the message of Christ's return (2 Pet. 3:3). The modern church must choose between having a form of godliness and denying the power (2 Tim. 3:1–5), or becoming a fire brand with a light burning bright. All of the above events and circumstances could overwhelm a believer and plant seeds of fear that breed the fruit of depression and discouragement. However, God never leaves a generation without a war strategy and weapons to win the moral, spiritual, and even political conflicts of their time.

## A View of the Last-Day Army of God

At the peak of Christ's ministry the multitudes offered to make Him a king, with the motive that He (through miraculous power) would defeat the Roman enemies. Christ refused, as the offer was useless and the timing was off. His kingdom message was one of deliverance from sin, sickness, and death, clashing with an invisible array of satanic rebels and bringing them into captivity to His name, His Word, and His will. His army was spiritual, with spiritual weapons and a sword of the Word. The same army exists today but will arise in the time of the end for their largest assignment in history! The prophet Joel predicted that in the last days God would pour out His Spirit upon all flesh (Joel 2:28–29). This ancient prophecy was repeated by the apostle Peter on the Day of Pentecost, when the Holy Spirit was poured out in Jerusalem. Based upon Acts 2:17–18, we see four important facts of God's end-time army:

1. The army consists of *sons and daughters* (v. 17).

2. The end-time army consists of *servants and hand-maidens* (v. 18).

3. The end-time army consists of *dreamers and visionaries* (v. 17).

4. The end-time army consists of *prophetic ministry* (v. 17).

This army has both young and old in its ranks. The older, mature generation has the *wisdom* from fighting *previous* battles, but the youth have the *strength* to fight *present* battles. Wisdom must be mixed with zeal, otherwise you will have needless casualties of war from fighting undefended without the weapons or the knowledge. The sons and daughters living today are marked as the final end-time soldiers.

The coming end-time army will be servants and handmaidens—those willing to serve in any part of the world and volunteer to minister to those from third-world poverty-infested nations. This end-time army will experience supernatural dreams and visions, which will provide them with warnings and direction to engage in conflicts and return with the spoils of war—souls snatched from Satan's domain. This army will also be a prophetic generation, geared to prophetic instruction, *hearing from God with a present truth for direction today and a prophetic truth for their direction tomorrow.*

The organizational skills of the Roman soldier's military units can teach the army of God much-needed lessons on the importance of maintaining unity for strength. In the Roman military eight men made up one *unit*, while ten units (eighty men) made up one *century*. It required six centuries to make up one *cohort*, and ten cohorts (forty-eight hundred men) were united as one *legion* (one legion could consist of up to six thousand men). When a Roman unit of soldiers joined together, they formed an effective and dangerous army.[1]

If we compare these military units to the size and strength of the various local churches scattered throughout North America, we see an interesting pattern. The *unit churches* would be churches with up to eighty members, and these churches exist by the thousands throughout rural communities and in small-town USA. The *century churches* would be those with above eighty and up to four hundred eighty attendees and are often found in smaller cities across the nation. The *cohort level* of forty-eight hundred attendees and above are the large megachurches that are usually found in the major cities of the nations.

Notice that at times the Roman military would join themselves together in larger groups to form one united, powerful group. The church's biggest weakness is that too often the body of Christ remains behind the four walls of their sanctuaries, with their own denominational flocks, and sees no need to join ranks with other Christians to strengthen the army of God. We spend so much time snuffing out the little fires in the church camps that we are too distracted to go after the huge fire that is burning the nation into ashes.

This lack of unity causes some ministers and Christians to become anti-denominational and preach against being connected with any particular groups. They see this "hiding under a bushel" mentality among denominational leadership. However, throughout history God has used particular groups to revive a lost or ignored biblical doctrine. Historically, denominations are groups of people under one leader who "camped" around or emphasized a particular truth. The Roman army was also organized into various camps, just as the body of Christ has camps formed around the main doctrine that distinguishes each group from other groups. There was the justification-by-faith camp, organized by believers who followed the biblical revelation that was revived under the leadership of Martin Luther. Following justification, there was a second reviving of the truth called sanctification, which was preached by the Wesley brothers, who organized the Wesleyan Methodist church. At the turn of the twentieth century a fresh outpouring of the Holy Spirit was released throughout North America, which birthed the Pentecostal movement, out of which came eight major denominations that camped around the doctrine of the baptism in the Holy Spirit. This was followed in 1948 with the Healing Revival and in 1967 with the Charismatic Renewal. Each revived doctrine or specific teaching marked the group that presented it to the world. All of these different movements in the Christian faith have proved the words of Paul: "But now indeed there are many members, yet one body" (1 Cor. 12:20).

## The Armies Rallied Around the Standards

It is difficult today to get numerous churches or denominations to join together as one unit for several reasons. One reason is that they have no specific leader who can rally them around one central point, unlike in the Roman time when soldiers rallied around their standard. The Roman standards (or Signum) were created as a long pole with various design elements created on the pole itself. Each standard was unique to the legion it represented and was carried at the head of the legion while on the march. On the top of each standard was a distinctive image; some had an eagle (representing the empire), a human hand (representing loyalty), and often an image of the emperor.[2] Two men were in charge of the standards, as this reminded them they were one army under one emperor and one empire.

The one standard of the Christian church and its universal emblem is the cross, representing the crucifixion of Christ, for through His death the redemptive covenant was provided. All Christians from all backgrounds should always be able to rally around the death, burial, and resurrection of Christ! After all, Christ was crucified upon a pole (tree/cross)—a straight piece of wood that is the *standard* of the covenant (1 Pet. 2:24).

Among the Romans the standards were used as a rallying point in the time of battle. The standards were where oaths were taken and renewed once a year. The standards were believed to embody the soul of the army. Biblical truths—the doctrine of the apostles, the instructions of the prophets, the words of Christ—should set the standards by which every believer lives. *The Bible is the standard that Christians globally should rally around.* When society challenges the accuracy of a biblical revelation such as the marriage covenant, believers must join ranks uniting under the standard ordained by God and fight the good fight of faith. We must *rally* around the cross, and we must *live* around the Word of God.

## THE GUMNASIA FACTOR

Paul wrote to his spiritual son, Timothy, and instructed, "But reject profane and old wives' fables, and exercise yourself toward godliness" (1 Tim. 4:7). The Greek word for "exercise" is the word *gumnazo* and is a word rich in meaning, especially as it relates to how a person trained for the games in the time of the apostle Paul. Among the ancient Greeks the gymnasium was not just the place of exercise and personal training, but it was also a meeting place where the men met to discuss politics and social issues along with the most important part of the exercising. In Paul's instruction to Timothy the word *gumnazo* was a word speaking of those who exercised in the gym. Paul, however, wrote that the physical exercise was of little benefit to Timothy (v. 8). However, Paul's instruction was for Timothy to exercise his mind, spirit, and emotions for the benefit of growing in the Lord. Paul's desire was for his spiritual son to learn to exercise the Word and spiritual principles that would mature him in excelling in godliness.

In the Greek gym the athletes were young men over eighteen years of age. Each man trained with the intent of winning the particular contest he was to be engaged in. In the listing of the armor of God, Paul said that we "wrestle." There were many different games in which men competed during the Greek Olympics or during the times of various festivals. However, wrestling is different because of three things.

1. You must always *face your opponent* and never turn your back, as if you turn, you will be slammed to the ground and penned in a dangerous position.

2. You must always watch and make eye contact with your opponent, otherwise a sudden move will be made that will catch you off guard, giving the advantage to your opponent.

3. The third aspect is that wrestling is the only sport in which you never lose physical contact with your opponent. Thus, wrestling is a face-to-face, eye-to-eye, hand-to-hand, and body-to-body contact sport. In the believer's case, it is not a sport but a matter of life and death.

In junior high school in northern Virginia I played three different sports: football, track, and wrestling. I tried out for basketball, but the other guys were just far better, so I never made the cut. Football practice was very intense and tiring, but I enjoyed the sport so much that I enjoyed the practice, knowing that each type of training would make me a better athlete. In track I usually placed in the long jump and high jump; I also enjoyed the training during the week before the competition with other schools. However, wrestling was the least enjoyable of all the sports. In fact, I eventually dropped out of the 135-pound weight group and retired for good from the idea of wrestling competition. In football, as the pace of the game picked up, you could at least get a break in the huddle and catch your breath before the next play. During track meets I would watch others, anticipating my turn in line. In wrestling the entire match was nonstop action—grabbing arms and legs, tugging, pulling, yanking, jerking—and brought misery when the opponent had you on your back and you were attempting to breathe with much of your opponent's weight pressing on your chest!

We know from Paul's revelation that there are four demonic competitors: principalities, powers, rulers of the darkness of this world, and wicked spirits in heavenly places (Eph. 6:12). Some of these spirits rule from the cosmic heavens, others on earth, and others through people. Thus we have conflicts above us, around us, upon us, and near us. These invisible yet tangible spirits and enemies of righteousness are experienced masters of lies, deception, and evil strategies. They have thousands of years of experience in dealing with nations, leaders, and common individuals. However, understanding how Greek athletes trained and seeing the parallels to our own spiritual wrestling will bring insight to help you better understand how to prepare for your ultimate contest with the prince of darkness.

## THE TRAINING OF A WRESTLER

Special gyms were assigned for training the athletes, and the wrestling schools were called the *palestra*. The root Greek word for *palestra* is *pale*, which is the Greek word for "wrestle" and the word Paul used when he said we "wrestle" (Eph. 6:12). The endurance and strength training were pivotal, as a strong opponent would attempt to wear down a weaker one. The wrestlers trained not only in the gym but also in their daily lives. Some were soldiers or did hard manual labor to build muscle and strength. Our daily lives must be a part of our training process—encountering different people, different religions, various attitudes, and observing the clash of the cultures all come into play in our spiritual equipping.

It is noted that the Greek word for "exercise" in the Bible actually means to "exercise naked." This is not an encouragement to become a "Christian streaker." I say this because some Christians only have on a helmet of salvation and have omitted the rest of their protective gear, walking into a battle without spiritual clothes. The helmet wearers are saved, go to church when convenient, and have accepted Christ only as "fire insurance" to stay out of hell. The warring believer, however, is to be covered with specific armor to prevent the hands of the enemy from gaining access to any part of their physical (through sickness) or spiritual man.

Each Greek gymnasium had specific trainers, many who were former, experienced champions who now trained the young men in the art of wrestling. The body of Christ must maximize opportunities and the experiences of retired ministers along with strong men and women of God to train and teach the younger generation how to fight, endure, and overcome.

Special hot baths and hot rooms were used by trainers to cause the wrestler to sweat. Hot baths and especially saunas are known to be good for removing impurities from the body. When we as believers are under a fiery trial of our faith, the intended outcome is to expose and burn out the internal spiritual bacteria and germs, killing them in us and removing any dangerous or spiritually unclean thing from our hearts.

There were also special rooms where the trainer took the trainee and would use different types of oils on the wrestler's body. These expensive oils made the body difficult to grip. As various types of grips and holds were used on the wrestler, his goal was to learn how to escape them, just as our goal is to escape from the snares and traps of the enemy. Oil in the Bible represents the anointing of the Holy Spirit. We must become so filled with the Spirit that we become *slippery* in the hands of our adversary. Satan had nothing to hold on to in the life of Jesus. Christ told His disciples:

> I will not talk with you much more, for the prince (evil genius, ruler) of the world is coming. And he has no claim on Me. [He has nothing in common with Me; there is nothing in Me that belongs to him, and he has no power over Me.]
> —JOHN 14:30, AMP

## CARRY A WOUNDED SOLDIER

One of the most unique methods of training, written about in an essay by Lucian od Samosata in AD 170, reveals certain aspects of the use of mud in the training process. In a conversational letter he wrote that the wrestler had mud covering his body in the training process. He noted that the wrestler was coated with sweat and mud, which to some seemed ridiculous. However, the purpose was two-fold. The mud, sweat, and oil made the trainee slipperier to hold on to and assisted him in learning how to maneuver out of tight situations. The other reasons given by Samosata was the muddy and sweaty body was good practice for a man to learn how to pick up a fellow soldier who was wounded in battle and required being carried, or to grab an enemy and bring him back to one's own lines. He wrote, "For such reasons we train them to the limits and set the most difficult task so that they can do the lesser one with greater ease."[3] All believers must be strong enough to hold up others who are weak, pick up others who have fallen, and help to carry those who are wounded to a place of safety and recovery.

When a soldier is wounded, there are two different things that can occur. Depending upon the type of wound, many times the adrenaline rush, coupled with inner strength and determination, causes a wounded soldier to continue to fight and engage the enemy. The more seriously wounded, however, must be carried out of the battle on the shoulders of other soldiers and placed on cots or in a helicopter. In the heat of a battle, when one soldier is wounded, if there is not proper medical help at that moment, it is possible that two other soldiers must assist in carrying the wounded one, which can remove two other fighters from the focus of the battle.

If a fellow Christian soldier falls away, back into the world or into sin, it always has an impact upon those who are closest to that person and can draw others out of their own present assignments as they go after the one who has fallen. Other warriors of the faith should determine not to allow a fellow believer to fall away and to be taken captive at the will of Satan (2 Tim. 2:26). Jesus taught that a good shepherd will leave the ninety nine and go after the one stray sheep (Matt. 18:12).

## GREAT TRIUMPH IN THE VICTORIES

The ancients were known for huge victory celebrations when a war victory was won! Through Christ's death and resurrection, we read where He "disarmed principalities and powers, He made a public spectacle of them, triumphing over them in it" (Col. 2:15). When Christ returns to earth to reign as King for a thousand years, He will arrive on a white stallion with all of the armies of heaven also following Him on white horses. The Scriptures reveal Christ's return to earth in the imagery of an ancient victory—a war celebration. There are several different parts of the ancient triumph celebration:

1. They rode in a chariot pulled by white horses.

2. They wore royal robes.

3. They wore gold tunics.

4. They wore crowns of victory.

5. They painted their faces red.

6. They held scepters.

7. They were surrounded by victorious soldiers.

8. The enemy was paraded around in chains.

9. The victors got the spoils of the war.

Notice the similar parallels in 2 Thessalonians and the Book of Revelation:

1. We will ride on white horses (Rev. 19:14).

2. We will be clothed in white robes of righteousness (Rev. 7:9; 19:14).

3. Christ will be wearing many crowns (v. 12).

4. Christ's coming will be bright—in flaming fire (2 Thess. 1:8).

5. Christ will rule with a rod of iron (Rev. 19:15).

6. Christ will return with the armies of heaven (v. 14).

7. Satan will be bound with chains (Rev. 20:1).

8. The believers will become the rulers, priests, and kings (Rev. 5:10).

When any believer overcomes temptation, sin, sickness, and fear and defeats an enemy, we should all rejoice and celebrate. When a ministry receives a financial breakthrough, instead of questioning, "Hey, God, why did they get that and not me?", you should rejoice in another man's blessing. When you are willing to rejoice in another man's victory, the time will come when they will also rejoice in yours!

# Chapter 15

# STRATEGIES FROM A
# WORLD-FAMOUS GENERAL

N ATURAL TRUTH CAN REFLECT SPIRITUAL APPLICATIONS.
This is true when comparing how strategies in a natural war can mirror the same strategies in a spiritual conflict. For
example, there have been six major empires of Bible prophecy:
Egypt, Assyria, Babylon, Greece, Media-Persia, and Rome. At its
peak each of these empires was noted to have both a strong military and strong leaders, each overpowering in war the empire that
preceded it. To me, the most fascinating was the Greek Empire
under the leadership of Alexander the Great. Without going into
detailed history, at age twenty Alexander began his military cam-
paigns, and by age thirty he had conquered and occupied all of
the Babylonian and Media-Persian empires. At age thirty-three
he died in Babylon, with practically no more nations to conquer.
He did great things with a small army. It is the fighting methods
and treatment of his army that distinguished Alexander from past

and future commanders. Each of Alexander's main emphases has a spiritual parallel for the church and the individual believer.

ALEXANDER'S ARMY WAS SMALL BUT MOTIVATED.

The Media-Persian Empire was ruling in 127 provinces at the peak of its domination (Esther 1:1). When Alexander and his soldiers set out to war against the Persians, Alexander took with him forty-thousand men and took on an army of one million. His men were so motivated that they swam across a cold river to attack the Persian army. This Grecian general may have lost five hundred troops, but the Persians lost thousands. In Scripture Gideon, an Old Testament judge, began with thirty-five thousand troops and was forced to reduce the numbers to three hundred when preparing to attack a large Midianite army. God, however, took the three hundred and through a supernatural act defeated a large army with a small group of highly motivated men (Judges 7–8). True motivation is not altered by negative circumstances, but it sees the challenge as an opportunity.

*The spiritual parallel*

Christ took twelve common men with common jobs and little or no formal education, turning them into a new nation called the church and a living organism called the body of Christ (Luke 9:1; 1 Pet. 2:9). In addition to these twelve men Christ appointed seventy to join in teams of two (thirty-five teams) and minister throughout Israel (Luke 10:1). On the Day of Pentecost three thousand new believers were introduced to the new covenant of Christ (Acts 2:41), and days later another five thousand believed (Acts 4:4). Today, those who claim the Christian faith are an estimated 1.8 to 2 billion around the globe. Alexander motivated his small army, and the Holy Spirit is the motivator for the individual believer to "wage the good warfare," and "fight the good fight of faith" (1 Tim. 1:18;

6:12). Our battle motivation is maintained through the belief that with God nothing shall be impossible (Mark 10:27).

ALEXANDER STUDIED THE WEAKNESSES OF HIS OPPOSITION.

He would spend hours looking for a hole in the defenses of his enemies. When preparing to advance upon a city, he took notice of any unguarded walls that could be a weak place for his army to capitalize on. He was also a master of using any type of fear his enemy had against them. The enemy's weakness became Alexander's strength.

### The spiritual parallel

When we are dealing with strong demonic forces, we often view this struggle as a tug of war, with God on one end and Satan on the other end of the rope. We often think that occasionally God gets the advantage, and at other times Satan drags God across the line. This is not the case. Jesus won the *war*, coming out of the grave swinging the keys of death and hell (Rev. 1:18), but we must win the *mini-battles* that are linked with being clothed in a human body and dealing with carnal people. The enemy has a weakness, and that weakness is that he can be *resisted* and *rebuked* through the authority of the name of Jesus Christ and can do nothing about it. If we submit to God and resist the devil, the enemy will flee from us (James 4:7). Thus resisting and rebuking are the weak spots in Satan's armor. When believers use the Word of God to rebuke and resist the enemy, it is as though the Lord Himself is speaking, as you have been given delegated authority through Christ's name (Luke 10:19).

ALEXANDER LIGHTENED HIS SOLDIERS' LOADS BEFORE THE
BATTLE.

While many modern soldiers will carry pounds of needed equipment on their bodies and in backpacks, Alexander believed you should not carry excessive baggage *into the battle*, as it would weigh you down, restrict your movement, and distract from the primary focus. Soldiers did carry large loads upon them prior to the battle, but the excessive weight was removed prior to the actual face-to-face, hand-to-hand combat.

### The spiritual parallel

The writer to the Hebrews made an important observation on running the race:

> Therefore we also, since we are surrounded by so great a cloud of witnesses, let us lay aside every weight, and the sin which so easily ensnares us, and let us run with endurance the race that is set before us, looking unto Jesus, the author and finisher of our faith.
>
> —HEBREWS 12:1–2

It is possible to become entangled with the cares of life and worn down with weights and burdens that distract you from the principal assignment. Paul advised Timothy about preparing for spiritual warfare with these words:

> You therefore must endure hardship as a good soldier of Jesus Christ. No one engaged in warfare entangles himself with the affairs of this life, that he may please him who enlisted him as a soldier.
>
> —2 TIMOTHY 2:3–4

As recorded in Mark 4:19, Christ revealed the three main weights that will bog down and distract a believer:

1. "The *cares* of this world"—distractions of various forms that weigh down your mind and oppress your spirit

2. "The *deceitfulness* of riches"—seeking after wealth, working to gain things while ignoring your spiritual growth

3. "The *desires* for other *things*"—meaning to covet and long after things, spending time pursuing after things

There is a difference in dealing with one conflict and in having three darts coming from three different directions at once. If you have a rebellious child addicted to illegal substances, a rough marriage, and lack of finances to pay the bills, then the burden and weight of the cares of life add on to the intensity of the battle. We must lighten the load so we can fight a good fight and come out without wounds and near-spiritual death experiences. Fight the most important battles first, and never let the enemy determine the playing field or throw unnecessary and excessive weights on your shoulders.

ALEXANDER FED HIS SOLDIERS WELL BEFORE THEIR JOURNEY.

There are so many believers, especially in North America, who are physically out of shape, and the junk foods they eat are causing mental fog, physical sluggishness, and even medical problems that are harming their bodies. Years ago I went from 225 pounds to 258 and felt totally out of control, tired, and sluggish. I finally decided to lose weight (about 40 pounds); I began exercising, and getting my body under subjection. This change in lifestyle actually made me feel twenty years younger (I said *feel*, not *look!*), with more energy and strength. It is impossible to fight a physical, mental, and, at times, spiritual battle without having energy in your body. Alexander knew that for his troops to perform at peak ability, they must be well fed. They all ate well prior to any major battle.

*The spiritual parallel*

In 1 Samuel 14 Saul was engaged in a battle, and his troops were hungry. He placed a foolish vow on his army demanding death to anyone who would seek out food to eat before the battle was over. Jonathan, the son of Saul, broke his father's vow; he dipped his rod in a honey comb, eating the honey and receiving strength (v. 29). Christ watched a multitude remain with Him for three days without food, and He responded by doing a miracle of multiplying bread and fish to provide nourishment for the people (Mark 8:2–9). When David was fleeing from King Saul, he was hungry and was provided bread by the priests from the table of showbread (1 Sam. 21:6). Our food must be physical for the physical man and spiritual (the Word) for the spirit man. Never quit eating the life-nourishing Word of God when you are spiritually weak.

ALEXANDER ALLOWED HIS MEN PLENTY OF REST.

I have spoken with men in America and Israel who fought in past wars. One retired Israeli commander of a large brigade told me something I will always remember. He said, "In war, your entire body goes into a different mode than at any previous time in your battle training. The fear is so great that some of the young soldiers are unable to control bowel movements. Their adrenaline is pumping, enabling them to go days without sleep, although their bodies do become tired and eventually exhaustion sets in. Once exhaustion arrives, it can be challenging for soldiers to think clearly and react sharply in a crisis moment." Any war will require, at some point, *rest* for the soldiers.

In the time of Alexander the Great his army averaged walking seven miles in four days. By doing this, the army was not over-extending themselves before a major conflict. General Alexander understood the importance of keeping the troops strong and refreshed at the same time. *A weary solder can eventually become a fallen soldier.* One of my dear friends, a minister, became so tired from several years of ministry stress that he reached the point where he said he could not even feel his skin. This was when the enemy struck him, when he was worn completely out.

### The spiritual parallel

Christ was an outdoor evangelistic preacher who taught and ministered to thousands each time His team (His disciples) prepared for a crusade. Jesus loved the people and refused no one who came to see Him. However, He knew when the physical man had reached its limit, and He took time to call His team aside and rest (Mark 6:31). Notice also that in the four Gospels much of Christ's personal prayer time was when He was "alone" (Matt. 14:23). Thus there was a time to be alone with God, alone with just His disciples, and then the time to appear before the multitude. If Christ required rest, then we too require rest.

This was one of the serious blunders made in the days of what was called the Healing Revival, a dynamic season in America from 1948 to 1955 when large tent cathedrals dotted the countryside and inner cities, bringing the message of salvation, healing, and deliverance to attendees, often with as many as fifteen thousand in attendance. It was common to keep the tent in one location for ten days up to three weeks at a time, with two and sometimes three services a day. On average, the night services would convene at 7:00 p.m. and continue until 11:00 p.m. or at times later into the night. After the service the evangelist would return to his motor home or a hotel and at times be unable to sleep at night, but he had to arise in the morning to be in the next service. This lifestyle opened the door to three negative outcomes.

First, because of the inability to sleep and the fact that there were no herbal vitamins and other nonnarcotic substances to enhance sleep (such as melatonin), some of the men, who were actually teetotalers (never drank alcohol), were given suggestions to begin drinking some wine to help them rest. Following this advice, two of the most noted men became full-blown alcoholics, with one losing his family, his ministry, and his integrity, and the other being exposed by the media. Instead of resting, they *burned the candle at both ends* and suffered the consequences of very unwise decisions.

Second, because the services concluded late at night, most of the ministers would *fellowship with other preachers* and *break bread*, either in a motor home, hotel restaurant, or the home of a well-to-do businessperson following the night service. The heat under the tent and long services released the appetite like a hungry beast looking for meat. I was told of one man who always ate a steak at night and another who loved ribs. The bad eating habits caused several noted evangelists to have heart attacks and die prematurely in their thirties and forties.

The third sad commentary has to do with why the healing revival only continued for about seven years. As with all sovereign revivals and historical movements of the Spirit, as long as the leaders remain humble and God sets the course, the ship will be blown in the right direction. However, as with most of the previous movements, pride and ego became stumbling blocks that eventually quenched the burning flames of revival and sent the men packing up their tents and hauling them into storage. One noted evangelist advertised the "world's largest gospel tent," causing a competing minister to customize his tent two feet longer, making his tent the *true* world's largest tent! Others would attempt to outdo other ministers in the level of the miracles being witnessed.

The lack of rest, the physical abuse of their bodies, and the allowance of pride to rise in their hearts, I believe, are three of the reasons this great outpouring continued only a limited time. If we do not learn from the mistakes of the past, we will repeat them in the future. Good soldiers must rest and have times of just "chilling out," as the kids often say. When we truly are at rest, then we cease from worry. Scholars note that an early Greek manuscript names a man called Titedios Amerimnos; his first name was a proper name, but the second name in Greek meant, "to worry." Based upon his name, it was believed that before his conversion he worried continually. However, in the manuscript, after being saved he became, "Titedios, the man who never worries."[1] When our body, soul, and spirit rest, we are recharged, renewed, and revived for the next season of engagement.

# Chapter 16

# IT'S NOT THE DEVIL—
# IT'S YOU!

I GREW UP IN A BEAUTIFUL RURAL COMMUNITY IN SOUTH-western Virginia, sitting in a church where my dad was pastor. One of the numerous, humorous memories was the testimony service, when the believers were asked to stand and tell something the Lord had done for them. Many times the words were brief, sweet, and edifying. At other times they could have been the main lines of a Christian comedy routine. One man said, "I always wanted God to make me a sweeter person, but I didn't know He would be killing me with sugar diabetes." At times the devil was blamed for busted septic pipes in the yard, a flat tire on the way to buy groceries, a neighbor who had hit the dog with the car, or varied negative circumstances. One lady stood and told how the devil had been riding on her back all day long. As a kid I thought, "What is this? Has the devil become a hitchhiker? Why is she letting him ride and not telling him to get off her back?" To some Christians, many of life's problems are blamed on the devil. In reality, however, it may not be the devil—it may be you!

The real enemy is often our *inner me*, or the internal carnal man versus the spiritual man. Paul wrote of our bodies being sown "a natural body" and raised "a spiritual body" when speaking of the future resurrection (1 Cor. 15:44). Among the Greeks, the natural man referred to the soul of a man, consisting of the five senses that received outward information and processed it into the natural man. The spiritual man is the inner spirit that gives man his consciousness of God and eternity. The Spirit world is invisible yet real and eternal in nature. John 4:24 reads in the Greek, "God is spirit." We know "angels are spirits" (Heb. 1:7) and all humans have a spirit (Heb. 12:23). Thus we have a physical body with an eternal spirit, which, if it departed from our body, would have the same basic form and appearance of our physical body, just like Moses's appearance on the Mount of Transfiguration fifteen hundred years after his death (Deut. 34:5–6; Matt. 17:2–3).

The fact is, you have a twin that lives within you—the inner you (2 Cor. 4:16), or what I call the *inner me*. That inner me can become spiritual or carnal; it can attempt to walk a tight rope between the carnal and spirit realms. These twins continually clash and create internal conflicts. There is a struggle between obedience and disobedience, between walking in light and in darkness, and desiring to do right and the desire to sin. Paul described the struggle between the inward man and the outward flesh man in these words:

> For I know that in me (that is, in my flesh) nothing good dwells; for to will is present with me, but how to perform what is good I do not find. For the good that I will to do, I do not do; but the evil I will not to do, that I practice. Now if I do what I will not to do, it is no longer I who do it, but sin that dwells in me.
>
> —Romans 7:18–20

You can be a Bible-toting, Jesus-loving, church-attending, tithe-giving Christian and still have that inner me enemy attempting to dominate and control your life. In this struggle of the twins, either joy or melancholy will dominate. Worship will dominate, or it will be spiritual dryness. In Gethsemane Christ asked His disciples to pray, and they all began to sleep. Then Christ revealed, "The spirit indeed is willing, but the flesh is weak" (Matt. 26:41).

Because man is a body, soul, and spirit, all three parts can be fed. The body survives with natural food and drink. Without natural food and water, the body cannot survive. The soul, or mind, is the intellectual and reasoning part of the human makeup and feeds off knowledge, images, pictures, and experiences; it is the place where wisdom is formed in a spiritually minded individual. The spirit of a man is the part that Christ referred to when He said to Satan, "Man shall not live by bread alone, but by every word that proceeds from the mouth of God" (Matt. 4:4). You will strengthen what you feed. However, not all types of food are good for the human body. Too much *fat* can clog the arteries and lead to heart failure. Wrong images imprinted in the mind from seeing or reading negative or perverse materials can build a prison of mental bondage that torments the person whose thoughts are filled with filth. The spirit of a person can be either spiritual through the amount of Word it receives, or it can starve and become weak to the point of spiritual death.

In what is called "the Lord's Prayer," the entire prayer is centered on growing in the Spirit and victory over temptation and evil (Matt. 6:9–13). In the prayer Christ prayed, "Give us this day our daily bread" (v. 11). This is commonly believed to be a prayer for provision, such as food. However, since bread is a metaphor for the Word of God (and for Christ Himself), including healing (Matt. 15:29–31), and Christ said He was the "living bread which came down from heaven" (John 6:51), the daily bread can also be a reference to a word from God each day that directs and sustains us. Just as Israel needed bread from heaven, called *manna*, during their forty years in the wilderness, we need a fresh inspiration and Word to feed our soul and spirit with every day.

## THE DIVIDED MIND

On Mount Carmel Elijah asked the people, "How long will you halt between two opinions?" The Hebrew word for "halt" here means "to skip over, hesitate, or to limp." Two opposing opinions in one heart will cause hesitation and bring a limp into your life. James reveals the weakening impact of being double minded:

> But let him ask in faith, with no doubting, for he who doubts is like a wave of the sea driven and tossed by the wind. For let not that man suppose that he will receive anything from the Lord; he is a double-minded man, unstable in all his ways.
> —JAMES 1:6–8

The King James Version reads, "Let him ask in faith, nothing wavering" (v. 6). To waver would be to say that you believe today, but then say that you don't believe tomorrow, or believe your prayer was heard today, and in three weeks question why no answer has manifested. Wavering is often caused by two things: a shifting in the outward circumstances that seems to indicate the opposite of what we believed for is happening, and when our emotions begin to fluctuate.

An emotion is a mental and physiological state associated with a wide variety of feelings, thoughts, and behaviors. Emotions are subjective to experiences, or experienced from an individual point of view. Emotions are also associated with mood, temperament, and personality. In the realm of emotions men and women are quite different. A man will pay two dollars for a one-dollar item but a women prefers to pay one dollar for a two-dollar item because it is on sale. A woman worries about the future until she gets a husband. A man never worried about the future until he gets a wife. Married men should just forget their mistakes, as there is no reason for two people to remember them. Men can wake up still feeling good about themselves in their own eyes, but a woman wakes up, looks in the mirror, and believes she has aged ten years in her sleep. When it comes to arguing, a woman (and I know this one for a fact) has the last word in any argument. Any last word a man has is at the beginning of the argument!

Even the language men and women use is often veiled. At times when my wife said *yes*, she was really saying *no*. Sometimes when she is hesitant and says, "It is OK," it really isn't OK. The statement "I am not upset" usually means "Of course I am upset; why did you even ask?" When men hear, "It's your decision," that statement ends up meaning, "Go ahead and do it, but I won't like it." If she ever asked, "You think I am gaining weight?," you had better change the subject real quickly and never, ever answer that question! Never ask a woman three questions: How old are you? Do you color your hair? Is your jewelry real?

Ladies, men also have their own lingo. When we say, "What?," it means that we're not paying attention at all. When we grunt out "Huh?," that means, "I'm not really listening." When we ask, "What did you say?," that means, "Could you be quiet?" If we answer with "Whatever," that can actually mean, "I'll agree with you if you will leave the room and let me finish this ball game."

Some of the emotional differences in females and males are seen below:

| Females | Males |
|---|---|
| Develop the right side of the brain faster, which leads to better conversation abilities | Develop the left side of the brain faster, which leads to better logical skills |

| Females | Males |
|---|---|
| Are interested in toys with faces | Like building blocks and challenges |
| Smile more and express happiness | Are more apt to act *macho* |
| Talk more about relationships | Talk more about jobs, politics, sports |
| Find security in friends, relationships | Find security in accomplishments, achievements |
| Will ask for help and information | Won't ask, because it makes them look like a failure |
| Will shop for hours | Will get what they want and get out |
| Are on average initiative, creative, integrative | Are on average logical, analytical, rational |

These differences should cause men and women to realize that their companion has the part of them that is missing and that the two halves joined together make one whole. Misunderstanding how a person is created, his or her strengths and weaknesses, can create conflict instead of resolution.

## PROBLEM SOLVING

There are five ways in which people deal with problems created by opinions, emotions, and conflicts caused by carnality.

### 1. THEY *FLEE* FROM PROBLEMS.

When Christ was arrested in Gethsemane, we read, "Then all the disciples forsook Him and fled" (Matt. 26:56). Following Christ's resurrection, they were piled up in a house with the doors shut for "fear of the Jews" (John 20:19). What they fled from was the possibility of their own death. However, what you run from you will meet again in the future. Eleven out of the twelve apostles who were present on the Day of Pentecost died as martyrs, including Peter, who died upside down by crucifixion. Your emotions may tell you to flee from a problem when your spirit will tell you to remain steadfast and unmovable, or as Paul wrote, "Having done all, to stand. Stand therefore" (Eph. 6:13–14). If you ever run from a problem, your reaction will be to run from problems the rest of your life, causing instability for you in other areas.

## 2. THEY *FOLLOW* AFTER PROBLEMS.

I have puzzled for years why some dedicated believers leave a good church with a group of cantankerous troublemakers who stirred up conflict and left a stink in the church they departed from. Does it ever come to a solid believer's mind that they may be following *the problem* and not the solution? After all, if a rebel and contentious individual is actually a spiritual "tare" (Matt. 13:24–30), then that person will never produce fruit, and by following a tare that has been removed from the field, the good "wheat" is uprooted and any fruit will die and wither away. Wolves will come in sheep's clothing, but observe their trail, and they still have a wolf's footprint.

## 3. THEY *FIGHT* OVER PROBLEMS.

A fight will always come to an end when one of the two individuals lays down his sword (bitter words), humbling himself, and either repents or walks away. But since no one wants to lose in a fight, two opponents just stand there and keep taking the verbal blows and sharp words, acting as though they are Ironman and Superwoman and nothing said will harm them. There are times to simply walk away and say nothing, because to speak will just create more problems. Solomon wrote, "A soft answer turns away wrath, but a harsh word stirs up anger" (Prov. 15:1). Also, "Where there is no wood, the fire goes out; and where there is no talebearer, strife ceases" (Prov. 26:20).

### 4. THEY *FORGET* THE PROBLEMS.

Some people walk away and act as if what was said or done had no impact upon them. Their attitude is, "Oh, just forget it!" However, the unresolved clash stays in the back of their mind. Others have an ability to let problems just roll off their mind and not dwell on them. Paul wrote, "Brethren, I do not count myself to have apprehended; but one thing I do, forgetting those things which are behind and reaching forward to those things which are ahead, I press toward the goal for the prize of the upward call of God in Christ Jesus" (Phil. 3:13–14).

### 5. THEY *FACE* THE PROBLEMS.

This is the only solution for maintaining peace and victory—to come face-to-face with your problem. A sinner cannot be saved until he admits he is a sinner. A sick person cannot be healed unless she acknowledges she is sick, and you cannot overcome a problem you will not face. I am quick to speak and think later, but I also know how to immediately admit when I am wrong.

## YOU AND YOUR TWIN

Two men in the Bible, Jacob and Esau, who came out of the same womb at about the same time are a picture of the struggle between the flesh and the spirit. Both brothers began their struggle against one another before their physical birth, just as your spiritual struggles did not begin once you were *saved* but before you were ever *born again*. The enemy tries to kill some prematurely through accidents, sickness, or addictions. After conversion we may struggle to discover why we were born and what our purpose is. You may wrestle over the idea of God's existence and the tug of war between faith and unbelief.

Ministers often refer to Esau, a red-headed hunter, as a man of the *flesh*. However, much of Jacob's early life was not an example of a picturesque spiritual leader. Jacob loved security. Esau, his brother, was an outdoorsman and a rugged man, but Jacob hung around the kitchen with his mother. Esau appears to have been a daddy's son and Jacob a momma's boy. Jacob also loved himself more than his own brother, as he was willing to manipulate his brother's weakness in order to steal his birthright and his father's blessing (Gen. 27:36). Jacob felt no conviction for using deception to get his way. By placing goat's hair on his arms, he was deceiving his blind father. Jacob's résumé would reveal that he had tricked his brother, Esau; Isaac, his father; and his father-in-law, Laban. For about seventy years Jacob lived a life of "It's all about me and what I can get"—until he hit a dangerous crisis.

After twenty years in exile, living in Syria and working for Laban (Gen. 31:41), Jacob returned to Canaan and discovered that Esau was bringing a small army to meet him. For all Jacob knew, Esau planned to assassinate him, endangering him, his two wives, and his children. There was nowhere else to run and no other relative's estate to escape to. It was time to come face-to-face with who he was, what he had become, and his pride. It was in that moment that Jacob had no choice but to wrestle! At times God allows trouble and conflict to come your way to confront you, forcing you to seek Him! We read where Jacob wrestled an angel till the breaking of day. In reality, the wrestling was not for the sake of the angel but for Jacob's sake. *Jacob had to confront Jacob before Jacob could become Israel.*

## WRESTLING HIS INNER ME

God's plan to build a mighty nation through Jacob's sons was already preordained. However, to bring the predestined purpose into the earth, this chosen vessel must be aligned in total right standing with God. Jacob's wrestling began late in the evening and continued all night until the sun was rising (Gen. 32:24–32). Three important things occurred in less than twelve hours, between sundown and sunup.

First, Jacob came up with a *plan* of how to meet Esau and protect his family at the same time (Gen. 33:1–3). When we wrestle with our inner me, removing spiritual hindrances, God will initiate creative ideas, spiritual strategies, and plans we were previously unaware of.

Second, the angel touched Jacob's thigh and gave him a *limp for life.* Jacob was a man on the run for many years, but now he could no longer run away from adversity; he was required to be totally dependent upon God.

Third, Jacob also received a major *name change,* from Jacob to *Israel,* the name ordained of God for the new nation promised to Abraham, his grandfather. The name *Jacob* in Hebrew is *Ya'akov,* from three Hebrew root letters: *ayin, kuf,* and *vet.* When Jacob and his twin, Esau, were born, Jacob grabbed the heel of Esau; the Hebrew word for "heel" is *ah'kev.* Jacob's name was given because of catching on to the heel of his brother at birth. Also, the three root letters in *Ya'akov—ayin, kuf, vet* (or *akov*)—mean crooked, or insidious, and the Hebrew word *aikev* means struggling. To Esau, his brother was a crooked deceiver, but to Jacob himself he was in a continual struggle, from the moment he wrestled in his mother's womb to the time he wrestled an angel. When the angel changed his name, he said Jacob would now be called Israel.[1]

His birth name was inspired from grabbing his brother's heel and wrestling in his mother's womb. His new name, Israel, was given because he had wrestled with God and prevailed! When forming an acrostic with the name Israel, and placing the Hebrew letter equivalent beside the English letter, we see how each letter is the first letter in the names of the major patriarch and matriarchs of the Jewish nation:*

- **I**—(the Hebrew letter *yod*), Isaac, Jacob, and Judah

- **S**—(the Hebrew letter *shin*), Sarah

- **R**—(the Hebrew letter *resh*), Rachel, Rebekah

- **A**—(the Hebrew letter *aleph*), Abraham

- **L**—(the Hebrew letter *lamed*), Leah

In the Hebrew, the name Israel begins with the *smallest* Hebrew letter, the letter *yod*, and concludes with the *tallest* Hebrew letter, the letter *lamed*. The concealed meaning is that Israel would begin as a small nation but would become a mighty nation, as it is written, "A little one shall become a thousand, and a small one a strong nation. I, the LORD, will hasten it in its time" (Isa. 60:22). Jacob wrestled the angel to receive a *blessing* (Gen. 32:26); instead he came away walking differently with a new name. Twenty years prior he left home as Jacob, with Esau threatening to kill him. Now he would meet Esau as Israel, one who prevailed with God.

For all believers *there comes a time when you have to step out of Jacob and step into Israel* by experiencing a God-encounter moment. How many times have you totally blown your commitment and knew you were out of God's will and away from His Word, yet God was merciful to preserve you from harm and danger? What is amazing is how God keeps His hand upon us because He can see the *other side of our heart*—the side that is pursuing Him. However, a divided heart will eventually lead to a defeated life with divided loyalties, and no person can serve two masters (Matt. 6:24). Our first goal in defeating our *inner me* is to petition God to *unite our heart* and not have divided loves, such as a love for people's praise and God's favor, or a love for men's attention and God's attention, and a love for the world mixing with a love for God.

> Teach me Your way, O LORD;
> I will walk in Your truth;
> Unite my heart to fear Your name.
> —PSALM 86:11

The heart is not just an organ in your chest that pumps blood, but it has an ability to reason, think, and sense emotion. There have been recent studies and books written on how heart transplant receivers have taken on certain personality and character traits from the person whose heart they received. Claims have been made that the recipient took on certain aspects of the donor's memory, characteristic likes and dislikes, causing a change in his or her own personality.

In published papers by Dr. Paul Pearsall, findings from seventy-three accounts from heart transplant patients and sixty-seven other organ transplant recipients were published. In most cases the recipient knew nothing of the donor and often had no clue who the donor actually was. One twenty-nine-year-old woman received the heart of a nineteen-year-old girl who had been killed in an auto accident. The recipient said when she got her new heart, almost every night she could feel the impact in her chest. She also began to hate meat, which she always enjoyed. The recipient confessed that she was gay but was now planning on being married. When researching the nineteen-year-old girl, her mother said she was a vegetarian and had a different man in her life every few months. After the wreck and before she died, she had written notes to her mother saying she would feel the impact of the car hitting her—she could feel it going through her body. While not all organ transplants have personality changes, there are accounts where people became interested in art, classical music, and certain foods that they previously had no desire for and even did not enjoy.[2]

The Bible has much to say about the heart, as the word *heart* is mentioned 830 times in 762 verses. The heart is also linked to the *mind* and *understanding*. We read, "Out of the abundance of the heart the mouth speaks" (Matt. 12:34), and "The heart is deceitful above all things, and desperately wicked; who can know it?" (Jer. 17:9). Christ said, "A good man out of the good treasure of his heart brings forth good things, and an evil man out of the evil treasure brings forth evil things" (Matt. 12:35). How can a flesh organ that pumps blood have the ability for memory or to inspire good or evil?

Dr. J. Andrew Armour, in 1994, wrote a theory that the human heart has a "heart brain." Consider that the heart has a detailed nervous system with forty thousand neurons. Dr. Armour believed the heart can act independently of the brain and can receive and send its own signals through its own autonomic nervous system. If so, this could help explain how hundreds of heart recipients received a heart with memory encoded that was capable of being transferred to them from the donor.[3]

If future studies can prove the heart is capable of memory storage and has its own *brain*, then it only authenticates what God has known from the beginning. Moses distinguished three levels where love is released when he said, "You shall love the LORD your God with all your heart, with all your soul, and with all your strength" (Deut. 6:5). Notice the Word of God discerns "the thoughts and intents of the heart" (Heb. 4:12). For many years I believed the biblical concept of the heart was a simple metaphor for the mind or the soul of a man, as the heart cannot actually *think*. However, there is too much biblical evidence that there is a special *brain* system within the heart itself that is capable of feeling, memory, thoughts, evil, and good. Scripturally not only must there be a fundamental change not only in the thought process of an individual, but also there must be a supernatural occurrence that transforms the evil condition of the human heart.

Consider the Book of Psalms. Most were written by David and mention the "heart" 122 times. Now consider the fact that David was a warrior from his youth, from the time he slew a bear, a lion, and Goliath (1 Sam. 17:35–36). David knew how to fight any enemy except the inner enemy that eventually struck him through the sin of adultery and murder. What is amazing is that David never lost a battle at any time to an enemy, and he always defeated anyone who came against him, often taking the spoils of the battle back home with him. The only war he ever lost was in his city, Jerusalem, in his palace in his own private chambers where one night became a lifetime of pain. David became his own worst enemy. Since the heart can be desperately wicked (Jer. 17:9), how can we experience a spiritual heart transplant, removing deception and imparting righteousness?

Through the experience of being "born again" (John 3:3, 7) God creates in a person a right heart and a clean spirit. Ezekiel described God's power to transform a person when he wrote:

> I will give you a new heart and put a new spirit within you; I will take the heart of stone out of your flesh and give you a heart of flesh. I will put My Spirit within you and cause you to walk in My statutes, and you will keep My judgments and do them.
> —EZEKIEL 36:26–27

In these last days there will be strategic warfare planned against the minds and the hearts of all believers. The helmet of salvation, the breastplate of righteousness, and the shield of faith will prevent the arrows, missiles, and other objects thrown our way from penetrating into our mind, heart, and spirit. When opposition, hindrances, and other challenges arise, it is easy to blame the devil for creating the havoc. However, much of our difficulty is the Jacob nature that must be wrestled out of us until we prevail with God and mature from infant knowledge to a mature and strong believer.

It has often been said, "Just trust your heart." However, Jeremiah 17:9 says:

> The heart is deceitful above all things,
> And desperately wicked;
> Who can know it?

If your personal life consists of fleshly sins, bad attitudes, and personal challenges, then your heart is the last thing to trust. If you live in the new covenant of redemption, and you are following God's instruction and obeying His Word, then He will direct you through a renewed spirit, mind, and heart.

Never blame Satan for your own personal choices. Never blame the devil when your will submitted to your own flesh. While the devil is called the tempter (Matt. 4:1-3), the strength to submit or resist is within the willpower of every believer. James wrote to "submit" to God but to "resist" the devil, and he would flee from you (James 4:7). The word *resist* means to stand against, similar to a wall that is strong enough to hold back the waves of a terrible storm beating against it.

At times it is not the "devil" in you but the you within you, the old carnal nature attempting to control the spiritual nature. However, through the armor of God and the weapons of our warfare, we are able to stand "in the evil day, and having done all, to stand. Stand therefore" (Eph. 6:13-14). The shoes of the Roman soldier had spikes underneath to ensure no slippage when confronting an enemy face-to-face. The God in you can override the flesh in you to defeat the enemies around you.

---

* There is no E in the acrostic because the English letter E has no Hebrew equivalent. In Hebrew, the name Israel is spelled with five letters instead of six.

# Chapter 17

# THE SEASON OF
# YOUR ULTIMATE TEST

THE NARRATIVE IS PERHAPS THE MOST UNUSUAL, AND TO the secular mind, the most ridiculous and inhumane story in the entire Bible. In the ancient story an older couple has believed for a son for many years. Now the man is ninety-nine, and the man's wife is ninety; she is barren and has already gone through menopause. By a miracle she conceives and gives birth to a son, and thus they held the promise from God in their arms. The boy grows up, and the father is told by the Lord to take this *miracle child* to a high mountain, build an altar, and offer him up to God as a sacrifice. (See Genesis 22.)

The critic questions, "What kind of God would demand a human sacrifice?" In answer, no one was actually sacrificed, as Isaac got up off the altar. To the believer, the question is, "Why would God give an old couple a son, then require the father to give him back on an altar of sacrifice?" The answer is that this event of Abraham offering Isaac on Mount Moriah in Jerusalem was a type and shadow, or a picture, of the future location and pattern of the crucifixion of Christ! Abraham was God's covenant man, and if Abraham was willing to give up his son of the covenant, then one day God would be willing to give up His only begotten Son as a sacrifice for mankind's sin.

When God was demanding Abraham to offer Isaac, we read, "God did tempt Abraham..." (Gen. 22:1, KJV). In English, when we read the word *tempt*, we think of "temptation." However, this word *tempt* is actually a Hebrew word for a *test*, such as to assay a metal by placing it under the fire. God tested Abraham's willingness and his faith in God's Word. The writer to the Hebrews revealed the level of Abraham's trust in God when he wrote that if Abraham had actually slain his son, this father believed God could even raise his son from the dead (Heb. 11:17–19). *God will never test you to give up anything He is unable to raise back up!*

We can certainly mark our spiritual, physical, or mental battles as a *test*. The word *test* is not found in the King James Version of the New Testament; however, there are two Greek words used in the Greek New Testament that carry the meaning of "to test." They are the words *dokimazo* and the word *peirazo*.

The first word, *dokimazo,* is used in an ancient Greek manuscript relating to a physician who had passed an examination to receive a degree of doctor of medicine; thus this Greek word refers to one who "passes the examination." Today in public schools and colleges we speak of giving the students a *test*, or in college an *exam.* By passing the exam, the student is approved in that subject. This idea of being approved or sanctioned is the meaning of the Greek word *dokimazo.* This word is used in the New Testament indicating the expectation of a good outcome as it relates to the test. One example can be seen in 1 Corinthians 3:13: "the fire itself will test the quality of each man's work."[1] When God allowed Job to be tested with the total loss of his children, his wealth, and his health, the Lord already knew that Job would not curse Him; God expected and planned a good outcome when Job's trial concluded. However, Job had to still *pass the test* to receive the double reward (Job 42:10).

The Greek word *dokimazo* is used of God and never of Satan. This word is translated as "prove" in the King James Version and is found in the following KJV passages.

1. In Luke 14:19 a man had requested to "prove" five yoke of oxen he had purchased.

2. Paul used the word referring to renewing your mind to "prove" what is the good, acceptable and perfect will of God (Rom. 12:2).

3. Paul wrote to the church at Corinth telling believers to "prove the sincerity of your love" (2 Cor. 8:8).

4. In 2 Corinthians 13:5 Paul asked the believers to examine themselves to "prove" if they were in the faith.

5. Paul asked the Thessalonians to "prove all things; hold fast that which is good" (1 Thess. 5:21).

In these instances when our faith, love, and mental thoughts have been tested and "proved," then we pass the tests and become "approved" of God (2 Cor. 10:18; 2 Tim. 2:15). The word *approved* is from the word *dokimos* and means "to be accepted after the testing." Surviving and overcoming a severe test from Satan places you in the category of an "overcoming" believer. The Greek word for "overcomes" (1 John 5:4) is the word *nikao* and means to conquer or to be victorious. The word was used among the Greeks to indicate an athlete who strived and eventually mastered the particular game in which he or she had competed. They were the champion of that game.[2]

The second New Testament Greek word for "to test" is *peirazo*, which originally meant "to pierce something with the intention to search it." It later came to mean "to put something to the test with the purpose of discovering if there is good or evil, or to discover if the thing had a *particular weakness*." There are certain items manufactured that must be tested before going to market to ensure they have no faults or weaknesses and will not break after the consumer purchases it. This Greek word indicates the type of test that produces such pressure that some men would fold or break under the weight. In the New Testament this word is used in connection with the tests and temptations that Satan brings, attempting to exploit the weakness in the person, breaking down his or her will-power during a time of physical or moral weakness. An example is when, concluding His forty-day fast, Christ hungered, and then the devil came to Him to test Him with food (Luke 4:2–3). Christ passed the test and ran Satan off the mountain by putting on His helmet of salvation, His breastplate of righteousness, and by wielding the sword of the Spirit. The devil departed "for a season" (Luke 4:13, KJV).

This is the type of test that Samson encountered as Delilah continually wore down his resistance with her words, weakening his will and finally causing God's champion to break under the pressure. He failed the test, lost his eyes and strength, and ended up in a Philistine mill house going in circles—blind, bound, and going round and round.

The word *peirazo* is used when Jesus was preaching to a hungry multitude and He went to Philip and asked him, "Where shall we buy bread, that these may eat?" (John 6:5). Jesus knew there were not enough stores in Galilee or enough money in the ministry account to feed this crowd. John reveals why Christ actually asked the question: "But this He said to test [*peirazo*] him, for He Himself knew what He would do" (v. 6). This was a test to reveal if Philip had faith or a lack of faith for a miracle. Philip was counting the offering and calculating the numbers, indicating the money and the numbers didn't add up (v. 7). At times we are tested, not to determine if there is good or evil, for the carnal man always has a tendency toward an evil inclination and must be brought under subjection to the spirit, but to expose a possible weakness that could later be used by the enemy to bring us down.

Another important place where the word *periazo* is found is in the Apocalypse, where Christ informs the church at Ephesus that He knows that they have "tested" those who said they were apostles (Rev. 2:2). These strangers in the church were to be put to a test by the believers to determine what was actually in their minds and hearts. We are uncertain what this test was, unless it was for them to prove and demonstrate the miraculous gifts as a sign of apostleship, which Paul spoke of in 2 Corinthians 12:12.

Another powerful example where this word is used is in Revelation 3:10:

> Because you have kept My command to persevere, I also will keep you from the hour of trial which shall come upon the whole world, to test those who dwell on the earth.

There is time of testing and trial coming upon the entire earth, to test (or "try," KJV) those who dwell in the earth. The Greek word *peirazo* is the word for "test." This testing is believed to refer to the Great Tribulation that is coming in the future upon the entire world. Here Christ promised to "keep" the church from the hour of testing. The Greek word for "keep" here refers to guarding something to prevent it from loss or injury; to keep an eye upon. This is the same Greek word used when Christ was praying for His disciples that the Father would *keep* them from evil and keep them through His name (John 17:11, 15).

It should be clear that there is a difference between a test that is permitted by the Lord and a test that is initiated by Satan. When God places us in a test, the purpose is to reveal the strength of our faith and to purify our minds and spirits by burning out the excessive dross that is in the precious metal vessel (2 Tim. 2:20). The test of Satan, in the form of temptation and harassment, is designed to make us fall into sin, lose our faith and confidence in God, and turn away from the truth. Once believers experience a "trial of their faith" and pass the test, they will emerge as gold that was tried in a fire:

> That the genuineness of your faith, being much more precious than gold that perishes, though it is tested by fire, may be found to praise, honor, and glory at the revelation of Jesus Christ.
>
> —1 PETER 1:7

When Satan set out to sift Simon Peter, Jesus revealed that an attack was coming; He also revealed He had already preceded Satan's attack by praying for Peter that "his faith should not fail" (Luke 22:32). The purpose of this attack was revealed: to embarrass Peter and bring such condemnation to him that he would quit the ministry and just give up. In reality, practically every attack a believer experiences in his or her life will in some manner be an assault against that believer's faith—what that believer says he or she believes in the Word and what he or she has taught others to believe. Satan enjoys challenging what God has said. Remember that the first temptation in the garden occurred when the adversary came to Eve and questioned, "Has God indeed said…?" (Gen. 3:1).

## FAILING A TEST

For years I have taught that testing comes in three levels:

- The *common* testing (1 Cor. 10:13)

- The *seasonal* testing (Luke 4:13)

- The *hour* of testing (Rev. 3:10)

The *common* tests are the everyday events that challenge our faith, patience, and determination to remain faithful to God and His Word. The *seasonal* tests are those trials and temptations that come in cycles, only to return and repeat over a set period of time. The *hour* of testing is the one major event or test that Satan determines to use to pull you away from God and your faith in Him.

The story of Job is a perfect example of a man who came under an hour of testing. Peter's hour of testing was an assignment from Satan directed toward taking him out before his future destiny as a leader would emerge. It was Peter who boasted to Christ that he would never deny Him and would follow Christ even unto death (Matt. 26:35). Peter proved his loyalty when he pulled out a sword and sliced off the ear of the high priest's servant. Christ rescued Peter from being arrested by performing a creative miracle of healing the man's ear (Luke 22:51). Peter and John then followed behind and gained access to the trial area. Peter was warming by a fire when he was accused of being a disciple of Christ. Fear gripped him, and he denied he even knew Christ (vv. 57–60). We read that on the third denial, "Then he began to curse and swear, 'I do not know this Man of whom you speak!'" (Mark 14:71).

To the English reader, when we read of Peter cursing and swearing, it appears that Peter went on a rampage of profanity. However, in the Greek New Testament we need to understand the meaning of the word *curse* in this passage. In Mark 14:71 Peter cursed and denied the Lord; the same Greek word is used by Paul in Galatians 1:9, where the word is translated "accursed":

> As we have said before, so now I say again, if anyone preaches any other gospel to you than what you have received, let him be accursed.
> —GALATIANS 1:9

In both instances, this Greek word for "curse" and "accursed" is the word *anathema*, meaning "to declare one liable to the severest divine penalties." Peter was not using profanity but was calling down a curse upon himself of divine penalties if he was not speaking the truth! Jesus predicted that before the rooster crowed the third time, Peter would have denied Him. Later, in Luke's Gospel, after revealing Peter's future denial, Jesus told His inner circle disciples in Gethsemane, "Watch and pray, lest you enter into temptation. The spirit indeed is willing, but the flesh is weak" (Matt. 26:41).[3] In the English language, the concept that Peter did use profanity in denying the Lord is suggested. However, this Greek word for "swear" in Mark 14:71 is the same word Paul used in Hebrews 6:13, where he speaks of God *swearing a covenant* to Abraham. The word means, "to take an oath," or making an oath. Thus Peter denied the Lord and announced a divine penalty upon himself in the form of an oath to prove to those present that he was not associated with Christ.

After hearing the rooster crow the third time, Peter ran from the people and wept bitterly (Luke 22:62). The reality of his failure and his lies overwhelmed him, as extreme conviction pierced his heart. Before this event Christ told Peter, "I have prayed for you, that your faith should not fail" (v. 32). Why was this prayer significant? In the time of Christ Jews took very seriously any form of a *verbal curse* that was placed upon someone or something, as blessings and curses were released by God Himself through either obedience or disobedience to the law of God. (See Deuteronomy

28.) Peter not only lied, denying he knew Christ, but also he had in reality opened the door for God to bring upon him a divine penalty. The disciples were warned of the power of words when Christ warned, "For by your words you will be justified, and by your words you will be condemned" (Matt. 12:37). In Peter's eyes he understood that his lying confession indicated he had *lost his faith* and was now under possible divine retribution. This was the moment that Christ had warned Peter about, when Satan would "sift" him as wheat (Luke 22:31).

There is no record of where Peter was or what he did for the three days that Christ was in the grave, other than when the Lord was raised. The angel at the garden tomb told the women, "But go, tell His disciples—and Peter—that He is going before you into Galilee; there you will see Him, as He said to you" (Mark 16:7). Afterward, when Christ arrived in Galilee and ate with His disciples, three times He asked Peter if he "loved" Him more than the other disciples, and three times Peter replied that he did ( John 21:15–17). I believe Christ desired for Peter to publicly confess his love for Christ before the other disciples to erase any *doubt* in their minds, any *guilt* in Peter's mind, and any *future condemnation* that Satan would throw Peter's way concerning his last failure. Through God's restoration process, failure is never final.

We are to count it all joy when we fall into "divers temptations" (James 1:2, KJV). We are told to rejoice when men hate and persecute us (Luke 6:23), and rejoice in "heaviness through manifold temptations" (1 Pet. 1:6, KJV). It seems counterproductive to rejoice when things are going bad (temptation, heaviness, persecution). However, it is the *end result* that matters, and when you fall into temptations, your faith is working patience, and patience will bring out of you a perfect work (James 1:2–4). The persecution is building up a special crown and reward for you in heaven (Luke 6:23), and the manifold temptations are the trial of your faith, which brings you forth as "much more precious than gold" (1 Pet. 1:7). Never look at the trials and temptations as defeat. Your ability to overcome always brings a great reward.

Much has been written over the decades related to the armor of God. However, I always sensed there was much more to this subject than what I had read or studied over the years—thus after additional study and insight through the Holy Spirit, I have prepared the book you have just read. It is my hope that each subject, paragraph, and sentence has produced a fabric of knowledge that has been woven into a covering of understanding that you can carry with you into any war of the mind, soul, and spirit. May I also suggest that you look at www.voe.org under our online store for more detailed resource information that you can acquire to tap into the deep truths of God's Word.

# Notes

## CHAPTER 1
### A REVELATION OF YOUR GOD GEAR

1. Rick Renner, *A Light in Darkness* (Tulsa, OK: Harrison House, 2011).

2. "Balteus & Ventralis—Military Belt & Waistband," Legio VI, http://legvi.tripod.com/id74.html (accessed October 25, 2013).

3. *Vincent's Word Studies in the New Testament*, electronic database, PC Study Bible, version 3.0, copyright © 1997 by Biblesoft, s.v. "Ephesians 6:16."

4. "Roman Offensive Weapons: The Sword," Roman Military Equipment, http://www.romancoins.info/MilitaryEquipment-Attack.html#Cingulum (accessed October 25, 2013).

5. Ibid.

6. Ibid.

7. Wayde I. Goodall with Rosalyn Goodall, *The Battle: Defeating the Enemies of Your Soul* (Lake Mary, FL: Creation House, 2005), 120. Viewed at Google Books.

8. W. E. Vine, *W. E. Vine's Complete Expository Dictionary* (Nashville: Thomas Nelson, 1996), s.v. "two-edged."

9. Ibid., s.v. "word."

10. Ibid.

11. MilitaryFactory.com, "Pilum Throwing Javelin," http://www.militaryfactory.com/ancient-warfare/detail.asp?ancient_id=pilum (accessed October 28, 2013).

12. This true story was related to the author by a pastor in Texas who knew personally the daughter to whom this happened.

## CHAPTER 2
### INHERITING YOUR ANCESTORS' DEMONS

1. TravelingHaiti.com, "The History of Haiti: The Haitian Rebellion," http://www.travelinghaiti.com/history_of_haiti/slave_rebellion.asp (accessed October 28, 2013).

2. *Time*, "The Death and Legacy of Papa Doc Duvalier," January 17, 2011, http://content.time.com/time/magazine/article/0,9171,876967-1,00.html (accessed October 28, 2013).

3. NPR.org, "In Earthquake Aftermath, Haitians Cling to Voodoo, Faith," January 22, 2010, http://www.npr.org/templates/story/story .php?storyId=122851808 (accessed October 28, 2013).

4. Several media sources have documented the curse placed against President Kennedy by Papa Doc, as well as Papa Doc's belief that he was "guarded" by the spirits on the twenty-second day of each month. See BBC .com, "1971: Haitian Dictator Dies," On This Day—April 22, http://news .bbc.co.uk/onthisday/hi/dates/stories/april/22/newsid_2525000/2525501.stm (accessed October 28, 2013); Col. R. D. Heinl Jr., "Armed U.S. Intervention Likely in Event of Duvalier's Death," *Virgin Islands Daily News*, 8, May 29, 1969, http://tinyurl.com/paurbfe (accessed October 28, 2013).

5. Kenneth S. Wuest, *Word Studies From the Greek New Testament* (Grand Rapids, MI: Wm. B. Eerdmans Publishing Co., 1980).

6. Perry Stone, *Purging Your House, Pruning Your Family Tree* (Lake Mary, FL: Charisma House, 2011), 19–30.

7. The author received this information verbally from Tony Scott during their theological discussion concerning binding and loosing.

8. *Vincent's Word Studies in the New Testament*, s.v. "James 4:7."

CHAPTER 4
BREAKING THE SPIRITS OF CUTTING AND SUICIDE

1. James Strong, *Strong's Exhaustive Concordance of the Bible* (Peabody, MA: Hendrickson Publishers, 2009), s.v. "NT:2896, *krazo*."

2. *Jamieson, Fausset, and Brown Commentary*, electronic database, PC Study Bible, version 3, copyright © 1997 by Biblesoft, s.v. "1 Kings 18:28."

3. Samantha Gluck, "Self Injury, Self Harm Statistics and Facts," HealthyPlace.com, July 4, 2013, http://www.healthyplace.com/abuse/self -injury/self-injury-self-harm-statistics-and-facts/ (accessed October 29, 2013).

4. Ibid.

5. "QuickStudy: Medical Facts," published by Evan Berner, http://www .scribd.com/doc/15723161/QuickStudy-Medical-Facts (accessed October 31, 2013).

## CHAPTER 6
### WHEN BELIEVERS BEGIN FAINTING

1. Rick Renner, *Sparkling Gems From the Greek* (Tulsa, OK: Harrison House, 2003), 557.

2. *Biblesoft's New Exhaustive Strong's Numbers and Concordance With Expanded Greek-Hebrew Dictionary*, electronic database, PC Study Bible, version 3, copyright © 1994, Biblesoft and International Bible Translators, Inc., s.v. "OT:2470, *chalah*."

3. Ibid., s.v. "OT:4805, *meriy*."

4. Ibid., s.v. "OT:4784, *marah*."

5. Ibid., s.v. "NT:1556, *ekdikeo*."

6. Ibid., s.v. "NT:4160, *poieo*."

7. Ibid., s.v. "NT:2896, *krazo*."

8. Ibid., s.v. "NT:310, *anaboao*."

9. Ibid., s.v. "NT:5455, *phoneo*."

10. One study that reveals the difference in emotional tears is an article by Jay L. Wile. You can view it at Jay L. Wile, "The Amazing Design of Human Tears," *Proslogion* (blog), January 12, 2011, http://blog.drwile.com/?p=3728 (accessed November 19, 2013).

## CHAPTER 7
### WHAT TO DO WITH YOUR BATTERED ARMOR

1. For more information, see the website for *America's Most Wanted* at http://www.amw.com/ (accessed November 19, 2013).

## CHAPTER 8
### DISCOVERING AND WEARING THE SHIELD OF FAVOR

1. Philologos, "Magen David: Shield or Star?," *The Jewish Daily Forward*, June 30, 2006, http://forward.com/articles/880/magen-david-shield-or-star/ (accessed November 20, 2013).

## CHAPTER 9
### MENDING CRACKS IN A BROKEN VESSEL

1. EngineeringToolbox.com, "Metals—Melting Temperatures," http://www.engineeringtoolbox.com/melting-temperature-metals-d_860.html (accessed December 4, 2013).

CHAPTER 10
DON'T GO TO HELL OVER A MYSTERY!

1. Finis Jennings Dake, "Miracles of Elijah and Elisha," in *The Dake Annotated Reference Bible* (Lawrenceville, GA: Dake Publishing, 1996), 394.


CHAPTER 11
GETTING BACK YOUR MIND WHEN YOU'RE AT WITS' END

1. William Wilson, *Wilson's Old Testament Word Studies* (Peabody, MA: Hendrickson Publishers, 1990), 485.


CHAPTER 12
WHEN A *SKANDALON* CRACKS YOUR SHIELD

1. One research paper on the capabilities of the heart is by Professor Mohamed Omar Salem, "The Heart, Mind and Spirit," http://tinyurl.com/yfpodcf (accessed December 5, 2013). Others may also be found online.

2. Preceptaustin.org, "Matthew 5:29–30 Commentary," http://www.preceptaustin.org/matthew_529-30.htm (accessed December 5, 2013).

3. Preceptaustin.org, "Romans 9:29–33 Commentary," http://preceptaustin.org/romans_929-33.htm (accessed December 5, 2013).


CHAPTER 14
REVIVING THE ANCIENT BATTLE STRATEGIES
FOR MODERN SPIRITUAL WAR

1. UNRV.com, "Organization of the Roman Imperial Legion," http://www.unrv.com/military/legion.php (accessed December 9, 2013).

2. LegionXXIV.org, "Imperial Aquila—Signums—Vexillium—Imago—Draco—Standards," http://www.legionxxiv.org/signum/ (accessed December 9, 2013).

3. As quoted in "An Ancient Take On Gi Vs Nogi," BJJMind.com, November 11, 2012, http://thebjjmind.com/2012/11/11/an-ancient-take-on-gi-vs-nogi/ (accessed December 9, 2013).


CHAPTER 15
STRATEGIES FROM A WORLD-FAMOUS GENERAL

1. Wuest, *Word Studies from the Greek New Testament*, vol. 3.

## CHAPTER 16
### IT'S NOT THE DEVIL—IT'S YOU!

1. TwebrewSchool.org, "The Hebrew Name Jacob," October 21, 2011, http://www.twebrewschool.org/2011/10/hebrew-name-jacob.html (accessed December 9, 2013).

2. Sabdeep Joshi, "Memory Transference in Organ Transplant Recipients," *Journal of New Approaches to Medicine and Health* 19, no. 1 (April 24, 2011): http://www.namahjournal.com/doc/Actual/Memory-transference-in-organ-transplant-recipients-vol-19-iss-1.html (accessed December 9, 2013).

3. J. Andrew Armour, "The Little Brain on the Heart," *Cleveland Clinic Journal of Medicine* 74, suppl. 1 (February 2007): http://www.ccjm.org/content/74/Suppl_1/S48.full.pdf (accessed December 9, 2013).

## CHAPTER 17
### THE SEASON OF YOUR ULTIMATE TEST

1. Wuest, *Word Studies From the Greek New Testament.*
2. Renner, *Sparkling Gems From the Greek*, 371.
3. Wuest, *Word Studies From the Greek New Testament.*